Derek O'Brien was born in Kolkata. He began his career as a journalist for *Sportsworld* magazine but soon shifted to advertising. After working for a number of very successful years as Creative Head of Ogilvy, Derek decided to focus all his energy and talent in his passion—quizzing.

Today, Derek is Asia's best-known quizmaster and the CEO of Derek O'Brien & Associates. He has been the host of the longest-running game show on Indian television, *The Cadbury Bournvita Quiz Contest*, for which he was voted the Best Anchor of a Game Show at the Indian Television Academy Awards for three years in a row. Always innovating, Derek is also credited with having conducted the first quiz on Twitter in 2010.

Derek has written over fifty bestselling reference, quiz and textbooks. In 2011, he was voted to the Rajya Sabha as a Member of Parliament (MP) and is the Leader of the All India Trinamool Congress Parliamentary Party in the Rajya Sabha and the chief national spokesperson.

Keep in touch with Derek on Twitter, where his handle is @quizderek, and on Facebook at www.facebook.com/MPDerekOBrien/

Other books by Derek O'Brien
(published by Rupa Publications)

The Bournvita Quiz Contest Quiz Book 2012
Bumper Bournvita Quiz Contest Quiz Book
Derek Introduces 100 Iconic Indians
Derek Introduces the Constitution and Parliament of India
Derek's Challenge
My Way: Success Mantras of 12 Achievers
Speak Up Speak Out
The Best of Bournvita Quiz Contest
The Bournvita Quiz Contest Quiz Book 2014
The Bournvita Quiz Contest Quiz Book 3
The Bournvita Quiz Contest Quiz Book 2017
The Essential BQC Quiz Book
The Ultimate Bournvita Quiz Contest Book of Knowledge Volume 1
The Ultimate Bournvita Quiz Contest Book of Knowledge Volume 2
The Ultimate Bournvita Quiz Contest Book of Knowledge Volume 3
The Ultimate Winning Minds Quiz Challenge
The School Quiz Book
Challenge Your Mind: The Very Best of Derek O'Brien

THE ULTIMATE

BOOK OF KNOWLEDGE

DEREK O'BRIEN

RUPA

Published by
Rupa Publications India Pvt. Ltd 2017
7/16, Ansari Road, Daryaganj
New Delhi 110002

Sales Centres:
Allahabad Bengaluru Chennai
Hyderabad Jaipur Kathmandu
Kolkata Mumbai

ISBN: 978-81-291-x x x-x

First impression 2017

10 9 8 7 6 5 4 3 2 1

CONTENTS

HALL OF FAME

PAST WINNERS OF THE BOURNVITA
QUIZ CONTEST

1994–1995, Mumbai

Campion High School, Mumbai
Balakrishnan Sivaraman, Sudhanshu Bhuwalka

1995–1996, Mumbai

Kendriya Vidyalaya, Powai, Mumbai
Eipy Koshy, Gourav Shah

1996–1997, Mumbai

Bombay International High School, Mumbai
Nirica Borges, Advait Behara

1997, Mumbai

Mount Saint Mary's School, New Delhi
Joe Christy, Maninder Singh Jessel

1997–1998, Mumbai

Bombay Scottish High School, Mumbai
Shaambhavi Pandyaa, Rahul Lalmalani

1998, Mumbai

Sacred Heart Convent School, Jamshedpur
Ela Verma, Lavanya Raghavan

1998–1999, Mumbai

Indian School Al Ghubra, Muscat
Anand Raghavan, Hitesh Kanvatirtha

1999, Mumbai

Maneckji Cooper High School, Mumbai
Ipsita Bandopadhyay, Gourav Bhattacharya

1999–2000, Mumbai

Chettinad Vidyashram, Chennai
Siddharth, Karthik Das

2000–2001, Mumbai

Bharatiya Vidya Bhavan, Hyderabad
Ananya Bhaskar, Aksha Anand

2001 September, Mumbai

Brightlands, Dehradun
Ankur Bharadwaj, Shray Sharma

2001 December, Mumbai

Little Flower High School, Hyderabad
G. Mithilesh, K Siddharth Reddy

2002 February, Bentota, Sri Lanka

G.D. Birla Centre For Education, Kolkata
Namrata Basu, Rituparna Dey

2002 June, Mumbai

Kerala Samajam Public School, Jamshedpur
Saurav Biswas, Kunal Mohan

2002 September, Mumbai

Jamnabai Narsee School, Mumbai
Sharan Narayanan, Vishnu Shrest

2003 January, Kerala

Naval Public High School, Mumbai
Apoorva Sharma, Abhishek Pandit

2003 May, Kolkata

St. Patrick's Higher Secondary School, Asansol
Pushpen Dasgupta, Shamik Ray

2003 October, Sangla

St. Agnes Loreto Day School, Lucknow
Aastha Srivastava, Illa Gupta

2004 February, Swabhumi, Kolkata

Apeejay School, Jalandhar
Mohit Thukral, Sahil Sareen

2004 May, Goa

Springdales School, Delhi
Anirudh Sridhar, B. Anuraag

2004 July, Indian Military Academy, Dehradun

The Mother's International School, Delhi
Krittika Adhikary, Milind Ganjoo

2004 November, Kolkata

Amity International, New Delhi
Aishwarya Singhal, Adarsh Modi

2005 August, Kolkata
Amity International, New Delhi
Utkarsh Johari, Aishwarya Singhal

2006 July, Kolkata
Riverdale High School, Dehradun
Kartikeya Panwar, Sumit Nair

2006 November, Kolkata
Seth Jaipuria School, Lucknow
Ratnaksha Lele, Ananya Kumar Singh

2011 August, Kolkata
Amity International School, Noida
 Kripi Badonia, Shinjini Biswas

2012 January, Kolkata
Birla Vidya Niketan, New Delhi
Anusha Malhotra, Nitya Bansal

2013 January, Kolkata
Vidyaniketan Public School (Ullal), Bengaluru
Shashank Niranjan Gowda, Mainak Mandal

2014 December, Kolkata
Centre Point, Amravati Road, Nagpur
Ratnasambhav Sahu, Tanaya Ramani

2016 January, Shantiniketan
Brightlands, Dehradun
Arhaan Ahmad, Vishwas Chawla

ART AND CULTURE

1. In 2002, who published his autobiography titled *Journey with a Hundred Strings: My Life in Music*?
   a) Ravi Shankar
   b) Alla Rakha Khan
   c) Amjad Ali Khan
   d) Shiv Kumar Sharma
2. In which of the following art forms are characters grouped as pacha, kathi and thadi?
   a) Kathak
   b) Bharatanatyam
   c) Kuchipudi
   d) Kathakali
3. Which of the following is a stringed instrument?
   a) Ghatam
   b) Mandolin
   c) Shehnai
   d) Bansuri
4. In Jainism, which festival commemorates Mahavira's attainment of moksha (salvation)?
   a) Diwali
   b) Holi
   c) Vasant Panchami
   d) Raksha Bandhan
5. Generally, Warli paintings are painted on a mud base using one colour. Which is it?
   a) White
   b) Blue

    c) Green
    d) Orange
6. Which modern-day instrument, according to legend, was inspired by the ravanastram, a stringed instrument made by Ravana?
    a) Violin
    b) Sitar
    c) Santoor
    d) Bagpipes
7. Who was the music director of All India Radio from 1949 to 1956?
    a) Zakir Hussain
    b) Bismillah Khan
    c) Ravi Shankar
    d) Shiv Kumar Sharma
8. Which of the following is a percussion instrument?
    a) Sarod
    b) Mridangam
    c) Sarangi
    d) Shehnai
9. Who sang as a playback singer in the 1956 film *Basant Bahar*?
    a) Ravi Shankar
    b) M.S. Subbulakshmi
    c) Bhimsen Joshi
    d) Zakir Hussain
10. What is the first line of a song or composition called?
    a) Alaap
    b) Mukhda
    c) Riyaz
    d) Sargam

11. The book *Bapi...The Love of My Life* is a daughter's tribute to:
    a) M.F. Hussain
    b) Shatrughan Sinha
    c) Ravi Shankar
    d) Pranab Mukherjee
12. Who received the Bharat Ratna in 1998?
    a) M.S. Subbulakshmi
    b) Ravi Shankar
    c) Bhimsen Joshi
    d) Shubha Mudgal
13. Traditionally, the white colour used in Madhubani paintings is obtained from:
    a) Milk
    b) Curd
    c) Rice
    d) Paneer
14. The Natyanjali Nritya Utsav of Chidambaram is dedicated to:
    a) Natraja
    b) Vishnu
    c) Kinnori
    d) Menaka
15. In 1973, who became the leader of the Tal Vadya Rhythm Band?
    a) Bismillah Khan
    b) Amjad Ali Khan
    c) Rashid Khan
    d) Zakir Hussain
16. Which of the following dance forms developed in Tamil Nadu?

    a) Kathak
    b) Bharatanatyam
    c) Kuchipudi
    d) Odissi

17. The archaeological evidence of which dance form, dating back to the 2nd century BC, is found in the Udayagiri and Khandagiri caves near Bhubaneswar?
    a) Manipuri
    b) Kathak
    c) Odissi
    d) Kuchipudi

18. Of all the portraits painted by Leonardo Da Vinci in Florence, how many survive till date?
    a) 1
    b) 5
    c) 20
    d) None

19. Which Bharat Ratna awardee played the shehnai in the 1959 film *Goonj Uthi Shehnai*?
    a) Zakir Hussain
    b) Bismillah Khan
    c) Ravi Shankar
    d) Hari Prasad Chaurasia

20. The book *Abba: God's Greatest Gift to Us* is about which classical musician of India?
    a) Bismillah Khan
    b) Zakir Hussain
    c) Amjad Ali Khan
    d) Rashid Khan

21. How is Tenzin Gyatso better known?
    a) Sunil Chhetri

    b) Bhaichung Bhutia
    c) Barack Obama
    d) Dalai Lama

22. Whose documentary, *Through the Eyes of a Painter*, won the Short Film Golden Bear Award at the Berlin International Film Festival in 1967?
    a) Satyajit Ray
    b) M.F. Husain
    c) R.K. Laxman
    d) Jamini Roy

23. Which of the following festivals is held at Kisama, about 12 km from Kohima?
    a) Hornbill Festival
    b) Bohag Bihu
    c) Nishagandhi Nritya Utsav
    d) International Kite Festival

24. Which of the following is a conical double-reed aerophone of South India?
    a) Nagaswaram
    b) Tabla
    c) Harmonium
    d) Sarangi

25. In which state is the Khajuraho Dance Festival held?
    a) Uttar Pradesh
    b) Madhya Pradesh
    c) Rajasthan
    d) Kerala

INDIA

1. In which language was the national anthem of India originally written?
   a) Hindi
   b) English
   c) Tamil
   d) Bengali
2. Ib in Odisha and Ode in Gujarat are:
   a) The shortest names of railway stations in India
   b) The smallest towns in India
   c) The largest towns in India
   d) The largest ports in India
3. Which punctuation mark forms a part of the logo of 'Incredible India'?
   a) Full stop
   b) Exclamation mark
   c) Semi colon
   d) Question mark
4. Which word comes from the Sanskrit words meaning 'bowing action'?
   a) Swagatam
   b) Shukriya
   c) Alvida
   d) Namaskar
5. In India, the number 102 is traditionally reserved for calling which of the following?
   a) The police
   b) An ambulance

    c) The fire brigade
    d) None of the above

6. Which post in India did G.V. Mavalankar, N. Sanjiva Reddy and P.A. Sangma all hold?
    a) Chairman, Rajya Sabha
    b) Chairman, Planning Commission
    c) Speaker, Lok Sabha
    d) Governor, Reserve Bank of India

7. If you were living in Mattur in Karnataka, which language would you be most likely to speak?
    a) Sanskrit
    b) English
    c) Bengali
    d) French

8. From which monument did Jawaharlal Nehru hoist the Indian national flag on 15 August 1947?
    a) Red Fort
    b) India Gate
    c) Jahangir's Tomb
    d) Parliament House

9. Which animal did the Royal Bengal Tiger replace as the national animal of India?
    a) One-horned rhinoceros
    b) Elephant
    c) Asiatic lion
    d) Indian spotted deer

10. How many digits are there in the Aadhar number issued by UIDAI?
    a) 12
    b) 14
    c) 16

    d) 18

11. What is the national heritage animal of India?
    a) Lion
    b) Musk deer
    c) Nilgiri Tahr
    d) Elephant

12. Of which festival does Dhanteras mark the beginning?
    a) Holi
    b) Diwali
    c) Guru Poornima
    d) Ganesh Chaturthi

13. According to the national calendar of India, the first day of a year in a non-leap year coincides with:
    a) 1 January
    b) 22 March
    c) 15 April
    d) 29 February

14. In India, nearly 90 per cent of which of these are located in rural areas?
    a) Headquarters of Indian Railways
    b) Banks
    c) Post Offices
    d) High Courts

15. Upon the members of which profession in India is the Sant Kabir Award conferred ?
    a) Fishermen
    b) Poets
    c) Singers
    d) Weavers

16. Which organization traces its origin to the Special Police Establishment that was set up in 1941?

a) CBI
b) RBI
c) NCC
d) BSF

17. In the Indian Navy, what are Rajput, Rana, Ranvir, Ranjit and Ranvijay as a group?
a) Horses
b) Destroyers
c) Fighter jets
d) Salute

18. Which state in India has the maximum number of districts?
a) Tamil Nadu
b) Uttar Pradesh
c) Goa
d) Manipur

19. Which of the following languages is *not* included in the language panel on Indian banknotes?
a) Bhojpuri
b) Urdu
c) Bengali
d) Tamil

20. Which of the following cities is so named because Lakshmana cut off Surpanakha's nose there?
a) Almora
b) Nainital
c) Nashik
d) Patna

21. What did Tenzing Norgay and Edmund Hillary leave behind on Mount Everest as an offering?
a) Pens

   b) Tandoori chicken
   c) Laptops
   d) Sweets

22. Whose birthday on 19 November is observed as National Integration Day in India?
   a) Jawaharlal Nehru
   b) Indira Gandhi
   c) Mahatma Gandhi
   d) S. Radhakrishnan

23. The motto of which organization is 'Bahujan Hitaya, Bahujan Sukhaya'?
   a) All India Radio
   b) Doordarshan
   c) Yashraj Films
   d) BCCI

24. According to the Shiromani Gurdwara Parbandhak Committee, how many Sikh gurus have there been?
   a) 2
   b) 10
   c) 11
   d) 12

25. Which is the least populous state in India?
   a) Goa
   b) Manipur
   c) Tamil Nadu
   d) Sikkim

MYTHOLOGY

1. According to Hindu mythology, what did Brahma create from Agni, Vayu and Ravi?
   a) The first three Vedas
   b) Tripura
   c) Shiva's trishul
   d) Saraswati, Lakshmi and Kali
2. Which character from the Ramayana was given his name by the devas due to a scar inflicted on his jaw by Indra's vajra?
   a) Sugriva
   b) Bali
   c) Hanuman
   d) Ravana
3. According to the Mahabharata, who among the following was Shakuni's sister?
   a) Uttara
   b) Draupadi
   c) Gandhari
   d) Kunti
4. According to Hindu mythology, from which part of Brahma's body was the sage Narada born?
   a) Ear
   b) Toe
   c) Thumb
   d) Lap
5. Whose first sermon is called 'Dharmachakra Pravartana Sutra'?

   a) Mahavira
   b) Buddha
   c) Guru Nanak
   d) Shankaracharya

6. In Hindu mythology, who was also known as Dasanana as he had ten heads?
   a) Rama
   b) Hanuman
   c) Ravana
   d) Garuda

7. With which religion would you associate the 'Guru ka Langar'?
   a) Hinduism
   b) Christianity
   c) Sikhism
   d) Buddhism

8. In the Mahabharata, who was Kunti's eldest son?
   a) Arjuna
   b) Karna
   c) Yudhishthira
   d) Nakula

9. In mythology, who among the following had the largest number of brothers?
   a) Lakshmana
   b) Bhim
   c) Duryodhan
   d) Achilles

10. In the Mahabharata, which modern-day city in India was known as Indraprastha, where the Pandavas lived?
   a) Calcutta

    b) Bombay

    c) Delhi

    d) Hyderabad

11. The name of which character in the Ramayana literally means 'furrow', as she was found by her adoptive father while he was ploughing a field?

    a) Urmila

    b) Sita

    c) Mandodari

    d) Mandavi

12. In Hinduism, what do the spots on the peacock's tail symbolize?

    a) Eyes of the gods

    b) Shiva's trishul

    c) Krishna's footprints

    d) Hanuman's teardrops

13. In Hindu mythology, who balanced the Govardhana mountain on his finger to protect his people from Indra's wrath?

    a) Krishna

    b) Rama

    c) Bharata

    d) Parashurama

14. In Hindu mythology, which god wrote the Mahabharata to Vyasa's dictation?

    a) Hanuman

    b) Ganesha

    c) Shiva

    d) Krishna

15. In Hindu mythology, whose devotee was Prahlada?

    a) Vishnu

    b) Brahma
    c) Shiva
    d) Indra

16. In Hindu mythology, who once wore a garland of consonants and vowels?
    a) Lakshmi
    b) Saraswati
    c) Kali
    d) Draupadi

17. With which religion would you associate a nihang?
    a) Sikhism
    b) Taoism
    c) Jainism
    d) Zoroastrianism

18. In Hindu mythology, who assists Yama by keeping records of the deeds of people?
    a) Indra
    b) Ganesha
    c) Chitragupta
    d) Brahma

19. Who was Dasharatha's first wife?
    a) Kaushalya
    b) Kaikeyi
    c) Madri
    d) Sumitra

20. In the Ramayana, venu, mridang, dundubhi and shankha were names of:
    a) Sita's sisters
    b) Musical instruments
    c) Chapters
    d) Arjuna's bows

21. According to Hindu mythology, which god is the creator of the universe?
    a) Shiva
    b) Indra
    c) Vishnu
    d) Brahma

22. In the Mahabharata, who was married to Hidimbi?
    a) Bhima
    b) Arjuna
    c) Nakula
    d) Sahadeva

23. According to Hindu mythology, who was the seventh incarnation of Mahavishnu?
    a) Krishna
    b) Rama
    c) Vamana
    d) Narasimha

24. Which Hindu deity is also known as Gangadhara, Chandrasekhara and Trilochana?
    a) Vishnu
    b) Shiva
    c) Krishna
    d) Brahma

25. In Hindu mythology, who constructed the city of Lanka?
    a) Vishwakarma
    b) Sushruta
    c) Dhanvantari
    d) Narada

POLITICS

1. In 1945, which future president of India, while working as a journalist, interviewed Mahatma Gandhi?
   a) Zail Singh
   b) Jawaharlal Nehru
   c) K.R. Narayanan
   d) Pratibha Patil

2. In 2005, who became the first woman chancellor of Germany?
   a) Theresa May
   b) Angela Merkel
   c) Dilma Rousseff
   d) Cristina Fernández de Kirchner

3. In 1984, whom did *Euromoney* magazine rate the world's 'Best Finance Minister'?
   a) R. Venkataraman
   b) Manmohan Singh
   c) Pranab Mukherjee
   d) Yashwant Sinha

4. In India, on 28 March 1989, what came down from twenty-one to eighteen?
   a) The number of states in India
   b) Voting age
   c) The number of cases of chickenpox
   d) National holidays

5. Which country's first woman prime minister was Khaleda Zia?

    a) Pakistan
    b) Sri Lanka
    c) Bangladesh
    d) Indonesia

6. In India, which ministry provides passports for citizens?
    a) Ministry of Railways
    b) Ministry of Textiles
    c) Ministry of Civil Aviation
    d) Ministry of External Affairs

7. Before the Supreme Court of India moved to its present building, from where did it function?
    a) Parliament House
    b) Rashtrapati Bhavan
    c) Red Fort
    d) Charminar

8. Who was the last governor-general of independent India?
    a) C. Rajagopalachari
    b) Rajendra Prasad
    c) Jawaharlal Nehru
    d) B.R. Ambedkar

9. Who has been the only woman finance minister of India so far?
    a) Indira Gandhi
    b) Meira Kumar
    c) Pratibha Patil
    d) Kiran Bedi

10. The national legislative assembly of Sweden is known as the:
    a) Riksdag

    b) Knesset

    c) Seimas

    d) Congress

11. Which leader's autobiography is also known as *Toward Freedom*?

    a) Bal Gangadhar Tilak

    b) Vallabhbhai Patel

    c) Maulana Abul Kalam Azad

    d) Jawaharlal Nehru

12. Of which country did Hamid Karzai become the first democratically elected president in 2004?

    a) Pakistan

    b) Indonesia

    c) Afghanistan

    d) Bangladesh

13. In 1966, who was sworn in as prime minister of India after the death of Lal Bahadur Shastri in Tashkent?

    a) Manmohan Singh

    b) Gulzarilal Nanda

    c) B.R. Ambedkar

    d) Morarji Desai

14. In which country is Sheikh Mujibur Rahman regarded as the 'Father of the Nation'?

    a) Pakistan

    b) Bangladesh

    c) Bahrain

    d) Kuwait

15. Who was the first vice-president of India to become president?

    a) Rajendra Prasad

    b) S. Radhakrishnan

    c) V.V. Giri

    d) N. Sanjiva Reddy

16. Who is the first African American to hold the office of the president of the USA?

    a) Thomas Jefferson

    b) John F. Kennedy

    c) Barack Obama

    d) George Washington

17. Which of the following countries had rulers primarily addressed by the title of 'Czar'?

    a) Spain

    b) Germany

    c) Japan

    d) Russia

18. Which finance minister had the opportunity to present two budgets on his birthday—in 1964 and 1968?

    a) Jawaharlal Nehru

    b) Rajiv Gandhi

    c) Morarji Desai

    d) Manmohan Singh

19. Which of the following is the samadhi sthal (memorial ground) of Jawaharlal Nehru?

    a) Shanti Van

    b) Vijay Ghat

    c) Shakti Sthal

    d) Kisan Ghat

20. Who was the first Indian woman ambassador to the USSR?

    a) Indira Gandhi

    b) Sarojini Naidu

    c) Annie Besant

    d) Vijaya Lakshmi Pandit

21. Till date, who has been the youngest prime minister of India?
    a) Lal Bahadur Shastri
    b) Chaudhary Charan Singh
    c) Morarji Desai
    d) Rajiv Gandhi

22. Which country's monarch is known as the 'Druk Gyalpo' (Dragon King)?
    a) Sri Lanka
    b) Bhutan
    c) Nepal
    d) Myanmar

23. Who voted for the first time in his/her life on 27 April 1994, at the age of seventy-five?
    a) Dalai Lama
    b) Nelson Mandela
    c) Mother Teresa
    d) Bill Clinton

24. Which Indian leader's wife is Gursharan Kaur?
    a) Pranab Mukherjee
    b) Manmohan Singh
    c) Hamid Ansari
    d) A.P.J. Abdul Kalam

25. Whom did Manmohan Singh refer to as the 'Bhishma Pitamah' of Indian politics?
    a) Mahatma Gandhi
    b) Atal Bihari Vajpayee
    c) Rahul Gandhi
    d) Himself

NATURE AND WILDLIFE-I

1. In India, what do the two breeds of goat, Changra and Chegu, produce?
    a) Pashmina
    b) Merino wool
    c) Silk
    d) Velvet
2. Which tree appears on the emblem of Saudi Arabia?
    a) Mango tree
    b) Neem tree
    c) Coconut tree
    d) Palm tree
3. Which is the only mammal that survives by consuming blood?
    a) Vampire bat
    b) Mongoose
    c) Polar bear
    d) Chimpanzee
4. Which tree is referred to as kalpa vriksha in Sanskrit, because nearly all its parts can be used?
    a) Watermelon
    b) Date
    c) Coconut
    d) Neem
5. The tail of which of the following creatures can break off and regenerate?
    a) Cat
    b) Iguana

   c) Elephant
   d) Rabbit

6. Which is the world's most populous breed of farm animal?
   a) Sheep
   b) Chicken
   c) Horse
   d) Pigeon

7. Which animal is the source of the majority of human rabies cases?
   a) Cow
   b) Sheep
   c) Cat
   d) Dog

8. In which Indian state is the Gir National Park located?
   a) Manipur
   b) Gujarat
   c) Tamil Nadu
   d) Maharashtra

9. Which of the following is *not* a reptile?
   a) Gecko
   b) Savannah Monitor
   c) Salamander
   d) Terrapin

10. Barasingha is a type of:
   a) Mouse
   b) Elephant
   c) Deer
   d) Lion

11. What is the title of Joy Adamson's first novel based on

the life of a lion cub?
a) *Pippa's Challenge*
b) *Born Free*
c) *The Searching Spirit*
d) *Queen of Shaba*

12. Which of the following animals is *not* a marsupial?
a) Kangaroo
b) Koala
c) Opossum
d) Gila Monster

13. Which of the following birds gets its pink colour from the shrimp-like crustaceans that it eats?
a) Ostrich
b) Crow
c) Flamingo
d) Hummingbird

14. The wings of which of these birds have been modified into flippers?
a) Ostriches
b) Penguins
c) Hens
d) Pelicans

15. At about six feet, which animal's legs are taller than many human beings?
a) Zebra
b) Hippopotamus
c) Giraffe
d) Bulldog

16. Which fibre is produced from the plants of the genus *Gossypium*?
a) Mohair

    b) Jute
    c) Cotton
    d) Wool

17. Which breed of dog can run the fastest?
    a) Afghan Hound
    b) Greyhound
    c) Dobermann
    d) Basset Hound

18. Which bird has the lowest body temperature of any bird?
    a) Ostrich
    b) Hummingbird
    c) Kiwi
    d) Penguin

19. Which of the following owes its name to the Quechua (Inca) word for the tree from whose bark it is made, and which means 'bark of barks'?
    a) Cardamom
    b) Quinine
    c) Nutmeg
    d) Penicillin

20. The name hummingbird comes from:
    a) The bird's call
    b) The sound made by its wings
    c) The flower it visits
    d) The place of its origin

21. Funnel-web, redback and brown recluse are different species of:
    a) Ants
    b) Spiders
    c) Snakes

    d) Turtles

22. Which member of the cat family appears on the state emblem of India?
    a) Tiger
    b) Cheetah
    c) Lion
    d) Puma

23. The name of which mammal owes its origins to a Greek word meaning 'a fish with a womb'?
    a) Octopus
    b) Shark
    c) Blue whale
    d) Dolphin

24. At which part of an enemy's body does the spitting cobra of Africa aim at?
    a) Eyes
    b) Neck
    c) Feet
    d) Ears

25. The name of which animal comes from a Sanskrit word meaning 'the spotted one'?
    a) Chital
    b) Cheetah
    c) Caribou
    d) Crocodile

FUN FACTS-1

1. The first words Alexander Graham Bell spoke into the telephone after he invented it were, 'Mr Watson – come here – I want to see you.'
2. Every tiger in the world is unique—no two tigers have the same pattern of stripes.
3. The word dessert comes from an old French word, *desservir*, meaning 'clear the table'.
4. The liver can grow back if a part of it is removed. It has the ability to grow to be just the right size for the body in which it is.
5. The Caspian Sea, the world's largest lake, is said to have been named 'sea' because, when the ancient Romans arrived there, they found the water to be salty.
6. Shah Rukh Khan made his television debut with the show *Fauji* in the year 1988. His character was named Abhimanyu Rai.
7. Adolf Hitler was nominated for the Nobel Peace Prize in 1939.
8. J.K. Rowling wrote books like *The Cuckoo's Calling*, *The Silkworm,* etc., under the pseudonym Robert Galbraith.
9. The first-ever YouTube video, titled *Me at the Zoo*, was posted by its co-founder, Jawed Karim, in 2005.
10. The Olympic Games were not held from 1940 to 1944 because of World War II.
11. Mimosa, a large genus of plants in the pea family,

is so named because of the movements of the leaves that 'mimic' animal sensibility. *Mimosa pudica* is a commonly grown plant of this genus.

12. Scientists studied chimpanzee behaviour to develop a humanoid robot named Nao. It can mimic the emotions of a one-year-old child.

NATURE AND WILDLIFE-II

1. Which reptile gets its name from the Greek words meaning 'terrible lizard'?
   a) Chameleon
   b) Dinosaur
   c) Tuatara
   d) Snake
2. Which of the following big cats cannot roar?
   a) Lion
   b) Cheetah
   c) Jaguar
   d) Tiger
3. Which country is home to the Sagarmatha National Park?
   a) India
   b) Sri Lanka
   c) Bhutan
   d) Nepal
4. Which of the following is the largest predatory fish in the world?
   a) Dolphin
   b) Blue whale
   c) Great white shark
   d) Swordfish
5. Which of the following products is obtained from a plant?
   a) Honey
   b) Silk

   c) Rubber

   d) Lac

6. Fire, pharaoh, army and carpenter are different types of:

   a) Spiders

   b) Cockroaches

   c) Ants

   d) Bees

7. The name of which animal comes from a Native American word meaning 'he who kills with one leap'?

   a) Bandicoot

   b) Jaguar

   c) Sloth

   d) Coyote

8. Which are the tallest of all marsupials?

   a) Kangaroos

   b) Koalas

   c) Wombats

   d) Tasmanian devils

9. The scientific name of which animal has the suffix 'unicornis'?

   a) Blackbuck

   b) Indian rhinoceros

   c) Hippopotamus

   d) Musk deer

10. The sword-billed species of which bird has the longest bill of any bird relative to its body length?

   a) Crane

   b) Kingfisher

   c) Pelican

   d) Hummingbird

11. Of which animal are Deccani, Chummarti and Sikang the Indian breeds?
    a) Horse
    b) Dog
    c) Cat
    d) Lion

12. Of which animal does the famous Kaziranga National Park harbour the world's largest population?
    a) Asiatic lion
    b) Indian rhinoceros
    c) Nilgai
    d) Gharial

13. Which is the only bird to have its nostrils at the end of its bill?
    a) Kingfisher
    b) Kiwi
    c) Crow
    d) Pelican

14. Which of the following animals can spend up to nineteen hours a day eating?
    a) Royal Bengal Tiger
    b) Indian elephant
    c) Asiatic lion
    d) Olive ridley turtle

15. Of which tree is *Ficus religiosa* the scientific name?
    a) Mango tree
    b) Neem tree
    c) Banyan tree
    d) Peepal tree

16. One of the distinguishing features that separate a monkey from an ape is that most monkeys:

    a) Have whiskers
    b) Have tails
    c) Are brown
    d) Move fast

17. Which of the following creatures has a species known as 'turban shell'?
    a) Crab
    b) Tortoise
    c) Oyster
    d) Marine snail

18. Which of the following national parks is located in India?
    a) The Jim Corbett National Park
    b) The Sagarmatha National Park
    c) The Yellowstone National Park
    d) The Serengeti National Park

19. Which of the following make up a quarter of all mammals?
    a) Bats
    b) Bears
    c) Elephants
    d) Orangutans

20. Which is the only bird to have two toes on each foot?
    a) Penguin
    b) Emu
    c) Ostrich
    d) Kiwi

21. What is the colour of a Komodo dragon's tongue?
    a) Red
    b) Yellow
    c) Green

    d) Blue

22. Which animal among all land mammals has the longest tail?
    a) Kangaroo
    b) Giraffe
    c) Elephant
    d) Zebra

23. Which of the following do not lay eggs?
    a) Mosquitoes
    b) Penguins
    c) King cobras
    d) Aardvarks

24. The lower half of the bill of which bird can hold about eleven litres of water, which is more than can be held in its stomach?
    a) Pelican
    b) Crane
    c) Flamingo
    d) Albatross

25. Which bird was once known as the 'camel bird' because of its long neck?
    a) Albatross
    b) Ostrich
    c) Crane
    d) Pelican

MATHS-I

Please go sequentially from left to right (not following BODMAS)

You can add, subtract, multiply or divide to figure out the correct answer:

								=	
1	35		7		14		11	=	8
2	27		33		2		8	=	15
3	47		15		17		1	=	49
4	60		26		5		17	=	10
5	35		3		15		21	=	28
6	65		25		8		11	=	55
7	46		34		35		5	=	9
8	15		4		28		12	=	44

THE HUMAN BODY-I

1. The size of which part of the human body increases during mental activities in proportion to the difficulty of the task?
   a) Finger nails
   b) Pupils
   c) Hair
   d) Teeth
2. Which was the first chemical compound to treat malaria successfully?
   a) Quinine
   b) Penicillin
   c) Petroleum jelly
   d) Neem oil
3. In 2015, on which continent did 92 per cent of all deaths in the world from malaria occur?
   a) Asia
   b) Africa
   c) North America
   d) Europe
4. In the human body, ball and socket and hinge are types of:
   a) Fats
   b) Muscles
   c) Joints
   d) Cells
5. With which part of the human body is prickly heat associated?

   a) Hair
   b) Skin
   c) Tongue
   d) Nails

6. Which is the most common reason for getting bilirubin levels tested?
   a) Jaundice
   b) Conjunctivitis
   c) Malaria
   d) Measles

7. With which organ of the human body is the pacemaker associated?
   a) Ear
   b) Heart
   c) Kidney
   d) Small intestine

8. In which part of the human body would you find calf muscles?
   a) Cheeks
   b) Legs
   c) Abdomen
   d) Fingers

9. Which of the the following is a fluid that contains white blood cells that protect against germs?
   a) Synovial fluid
   b) Lymph
   c) Vitreous humour
   d) Meninges

10. Which vitamin is required by the human body to heal wounds and repair cartilage, bones and teeth?
   a) Vitamin A

   b) Vitamin B
   c) Vitamin C
   d) Vitamin D
11. Which of the following shares its name with a bone in the human body?
   a) Diameter
   b) Radius
   c) Hypotenuse
   d) Perimeter
12. Parkinson's disease is a progressive disorder of the:
   a) Digestive system
   b) Circulatory system
   c) Urinary system
   d) Nervous system
13. Which is the most commonly transplanted organ in the human body?
   a) Liver
   b) Ear
   c) Kidney
   d) Lung
14. Which part of the human body secretes hydrochloric acid to kill the bacteria in food?
   a) Liver
   b) Stomach
   c) Small intestine
   d) Pancreas
15. Medulla oblongata is the lowest part of the:
   a) Brain
   b) Kidney
   c) Liver
   d) Nose

16. Which structure in the human body is surrounded by periodontal tissues?
    a) Heart
    b) Teeth
    c) Lungs
    d) Liver
17. The islets of Langerhans are embedded in the:
    a) Pancreas
    b) Kidney
    c) Liver
    d) Spleen
18. In which organ is bile, a greenish-yellow secretion, produced?
    a) Liver
    b) Lungs
    c) Heart
    d) Pancreas
19. Of which part of the human body are the antrum and the pylorus the regions?
    a) Stomach
    b) Gall bladder
    c) Liver
    d) Lungs
20. Which part of the human body contains about one hundred million photoreceptors?
    a) Tongue
    b) Nose
    c) Eye
    d) Ear
21. The coccyx is found at the base of the:
    a) Tongue

b) Vertebral column
c) Small intestine
d) Brain

22. MMR is a safe combined vaccine that protects against measles, rubella and which other disease?
a) Mumps
b) Malaria
c) Muscular Dystrophy
d) Meningitis

23. Which of the following words is associated with the region immediately beneath the skin?
a) Hypodermic
b) Haemophilia
c) Dementia
d) Vaccination

24. Villi are finger-like projections of the lining of the:
a) Lungs
b) Tongue
c) Small intestine
d) Kidney

25. A1C is a laboratory test that shows the average level of what over the previous three months?
a) Protein
b) Creatinine
c) Urea
d) Blood sugar

FUN FACTS-2

1. The Queen of the Andes (*puya raimondii* in Spanish) plant blooms only once every eighty or more years.
2. Neil Papworth, British software architect, designer and developer, sent the first-ever text message on 3 December 1992. It read, 'Merry Christmas'.
3. The construction of Taj Mahal was started in AD 1632 and completed in AD 1648. Twenty thousand workmen are said to have been employed for approximately twenty years on a daily basis.
4. Lionel Messi, widely regarded as one of the greatest players of the modern generation, was shown the red card on his international debut at the age of 18, in the year 2005.
5. By the age of five or six, the human brain is about 90 per cent of its adult size.
6. The book *Treasure Island* was inspired by a map of an imaginary, romantic island that author R.L. Stevenson idly drew with his stepson on a rainy day.
7. The 2010 movie *The Social Network* is based on the life of Facebook co-founder Mark Zuckerberg.
8. The Latin name for the cacao tree, Theobroma cacao, means 'food of the gods'.
9. The word 'Malayalam' is an example of a palindrome—a word or a phrase that reads the same backwards as forwards.
10. In 2011, Asha Bhosle entered the Guinness World Records for the largest number of studio recordings.

She had recorded 11,000 solo, duet and chorus-backed songs, in over twenty Indian languages since 1947.

11. The sun is about 99.86 per cent of the total mass of the solar system.

12. Penguins cannot fly. They use their wings, called flippers, to push their bodies forward while moving underwater.

GENERAL-I

1. Weighing only 0.03 grams, Treskilling Yellow is thought to be the most valuable thing in existence by weight and volume. What is it?
   a) A stamp
   b) A needle
   c) A coin
   d) A nail
2. What is the official religion of Cambodia?
   a) Buddhism
   b) Sikhism
   c) Jainism
   d) Zoroastrianism
3. Which feat connects James Irwin, David Scott and Alan Shepard?
   a) Climbing Mount Everest
   b) Landing on the moon
   c) Reaching the North Pole
   d) Discovering Antarctica
4. Which country has changed its national flag the most number of times in the 20th century?
   a) Afghanistan
   b) Sri Lanka
   c) Nepal
   d) USA
5. In which profession would you be if you wore a *toque blanche*?
   a) Doctor

    b) Lawyer
    c) Chef
    d) Policeman

6. Which term is derived from a Greek word meaning 'number'?
    a) Astronomy
    b) Arithmetic
    c) Mensuration
    d) Algebra

7. Of which variety is the bulk of the silk produced in the world?
    a) Eri
    b) Tussar
    c) Mulberry
    d) Muga

8. Of which of the following countries are the garuda (a mythical half-man, half-bird figure) and the elephant the national symbols?
    a) Japan
    b) Thailand
    c) Pakistan
    d) Bangladesh

9. Nelson Mandela said, '_______ is the most powerful weapon which you can use to change the world.' Fill in the blank.
    a) Imagination
    b) Perseverance
    c) Education
    d) Action

10. With which country would you associate ikebana, the art of flower arrangement?

    a) Japan
    b) Germany
    c) Nepal
    d) Thailand

11. Which of these values is equal to 10 lakhs?
    a) 1 million
    b) 10 million
    c) 100 million
    d) 1 billion

12. How many sides does a dodecagon have?
    a) 3
    b) 12
    c) 17
    d) 30

13. Which famous ruler's tomb lies at Mohalla Bulbuli Khana in Old Delhi?
    a) Razia Sultan
    b) Bahadur Shah Zafar
    c) Shah Jahan
    d) Rani of Jhansi

14. Which of the following can be used to remove ink stains from coloured clothes?
    a) Coconut water
    b) Mustard oil
    c) Honey
    d) Milk

15. Of which metal are the bells on ghungroos usually made?
    a) Silver
    b) Brass
    c) Copper

    d) Iron

16. Which colour is common to the flags of Bangladesh, Switzerland and Japan?
    a) Green
    b) Red
    c) Orange
    d) White

17. To which state of India is the dance form Kuchipudi indigenous?
    a) Kerala
    b) Andhra Pradesh
    c) Odisha
    d) Tamil Nadu

18. With which state in India would you associate Warli folk paintings?
    a) Maharashtra
    b) Gujarat
    c) Rajasthan
    d) Karnataka

19. Who became the first Asian to win the Nobel Prize for Physics in 1930?
    a) Amartya Sen
    b) Salman Rushdie
    c) C.V. Raman
    d) V. Ramakrishnan

20. Which of the following is an Indian word for 100 lakhs?
    a) Crore
    b) Million
    c) Kosh
    d) Rati

21. Which precious stone owes its origin to the Latin word for 'seawater'?
    a) Turquoise
    b) Aquamarine
    c) Emerald
    d) Topaz
22. Of what are log, yearner, soldier, freefall and starfish different types?
    a) Fictional warriors
    b) Types of cakes
    c) Types of moustaches
    d) Sleeping positions
23. All new euro banknotes feature the name of the currency in Latin, Cyrillic and _______ .
    a) Greek
    b) French
    c) Arabic
    d) Hebrew
24. Who signs the Bharat Ratna certificate?
    a) The prime minister of India
    b) The president of India
    c) No one
    d) The chief justice of India
25. What, apart from white, is the official colour of Canada?
    a) Yellow
    b) Red
    c) Orange
    d) Blue

MATHS-II

Please go sequentially from left to right (not following BODMAS)
You can add, subtract, multiply or divide to figure out the correct answer:

1	7	9	32	18	= 49
2	34	5	16	31	= 6
3	49	7	83	0	= 0
4	74	46	6	11	= 9
5	39	13	95	69	= 29
6	5	97	54	3	= 16
7	84	13	88	9	= 81
8	85	5	25	23	= 19

GENERAL-II

1. The flag of which of the following countries features a yellow sun with a human face known as 'the Sun of May'?
   a) Japan
   b) Argentina
   c) Bangladesh
   d) Brazil

2. Which was the first Indian couple to feature on an Indian postage stamp after Independence?
   a) Mahatma and Kasturba Gandhi
   b) Jawaharlal and Kamala Nehru
   c) Sachin and Anjali Tendulkar
   d) No couple

3. Of what are Trinidad Scorpion 'Butch T' pepper, Bhut Jolokia and Naga Viper pepper varieties?
   a) Snakes
   b) Chillies
   c) Islands
   d) Hats

4. Which of the following Nobel Laureates was not born in India?
   a) Ronald Ross
   b) Rudyard Kipling
   c) Mother Teresa
   d) Amartya Sen

5. Around AD 550, what did the Byzantine (East Roman) Emperor Justinian I persuade two Persian

monks from China to smuggle to Constantinople in the hollows of their bamboo canes?

a) Tea leaves
b) Papyrus
c) Leather shoes
d) Silkworm eggs

6. In which Indian state is the largest number of jute mills located?

a) West Bengal
b) Kerala
c) Assam
d) Bihar

7. How many times does the letter C appear while writing from 1 to 100 in words?

a) Never
b) 2 times
c) 23 times
d) 100 times

8. Which of the following is named after the president of a country?

a) The Ramon Magsaysay Award
b) The Fields Medal
c) The Pulitzer Prize
d) The Man Booker Prize

9. Of which of the following countries is 'Marcha Real' the national anthem?

a. USA
b. Spain
c. Bangladesh
d. United Kingdom

10. Who was awarded the Nobel Peace Prize in 1991 but

gave the acceptance speech only in 2012?
a) Nelson Mandela
b) Aung San Suu Kyi
c) Amartya Sen
d) Angela Merkel

11. If you subtracted 100 lakhs from 1 crore, what would you be left with?
a) Zero
b) 10,000
c) 1 lakh
d) 1 million

12. The name of which gemstone comes from a Greek word meaning, 'invincible'?
a) Pearl
b) Ruby
c) Diamond
d) Sapphire

13. According to the Chinese calendar, of which animal or reptile was 2013 (starting on 10 February of the Gregorian calendar) the year?
a) Snake
b) Rabbit
c) Rat
d) Horse

14. Till 2016, apart from Sir C.V. Raman and A.P.J. Abdul Kalam, who is the only other person to have been awarded the Bharat Ratna for his contribution to science?
a) Homi Bhabha
b) C.N.R. Rao
c) Jagadish Chandra Bose

    d) Vikram Sarabhai

15. In which of these countries was television introduced in 1999?
    a) USA
    b) UAE
    c) Bhutan
    d) Bangladesh

16. Of what are pencil, toothbrush and handlebar different kinds?
    a) Skirts
    b) Moustaches
    c) Heels
    d) Hairstyles

17. What connects Gharchola and Paithani?
    a) Bags
    b) Sarees
    c) Bangles
    d) Shoes

18. Who received his first nomination for the Nobel Prize for Literature in 1933 and his last nomination in the category in 1963?
    a) Jawaharlal Nehru
    b) C. Rajagopalachari
    c) S. Radhakrishnan
    d) Atal Bihari Vajpayee

19. Natural teak forests grow in Laos, Myanmar, Thailand and which other country?
    a) China
    b) Sri Lanka
    c) India
    d) Japan

20. What does 'L' stand for in the acronym ILO?
    a) Legal
    b) Labour
    c) Literary
    d) Livelihood
21. Which was the first YouTube video to hit more than one billion likes?
    a) Obama victory speech
    b) Usain Bolt 100 m sprint
    c) Curiosity on Mars
    d) Gangnam Style
22. Who received the Dadasaheb Phalke Award in 2007?
    a) Shyam Benegal
    b) Manna Dey
    c) Mrinal Sen
    d) Asha Bhosle
23. Arches, whorls, simple loops and double loops are patterns of:
    a) Leaves
    b) Fingerprints
    c) Sand dunes
    d) Corals
24. Sherpas are known for their skill in:
    a) Breeding camels
    b) Sword fighting
    c) Mountaineering
    d) Scuba diving
25. The four flags planted by Tenzing Norgay and Edmund Hillary on Mount Everest were those of the UK, Nepal, India and the:
    a) United Nations

b) Greenpeace
c) World Health Organization
d) European Union

FUN FACTS-3

1. Only two elements are liquid at room temperature, approximately 25°C—mercury and bromine.
2. *Ben-Hur, Titanic* and *The Lord of the Rings: The Return of the King,* all have won 11 Oscars each—the most won by any film till 2016.
3. One drop of blood contains about 10,000 white blood cells and 250,000 platelets.
4. The name of the Chinese dish dim sum comes from two Chinese words meaning 'dot' and 'heart'.
5. Tamil is one of the official languages of Singapore and, in Sri Lanka, it is an official as well as the national language.
6. Google names all its Android versions after desserts in alphabetical order. Some of the versions are Cupcake, Donut, Eclair, Froyo, Gingerbread, etc.
7. Sachin Tendulkar has received the Rajiv Gandhi Khel Ratna, the Arjuna Award for Cricket and the Padma Shri—the only cricketer to have received all three of them.
8. The full name of the Statue of Liberty is 'Liberty Enlightening the World'. It was gifted by France to America in 1886.
9. In 1964, William Shakespeare became the first non-Royal to be shown on a UK postage stamp.
10. In 2011, Scrooge McDuck was named the richest fictional character in the world by *Forbes* magazine.
11. According to the Flag Code of India, the national flag

of India has to be rectangular in shape and the ratio of the length to the height of the flag has to be 3:2.

12. Amartya Sen is the first Asian to have received the Nobel Prize in Economic Sciences.

HISTORY-I

1. Which of the following was *not* built by Shah Jahan?
   a) Red Fort
   b) Taj Mahal
   c) Jama Masjid
   d) Qutb Minar
2. Which of the following took the longest to build?
   a) Taj Mahal
   b) Commonwealth Village
   c) Hawa Mahal
   d) Parliament House
3. Which famous person was born in the Shivneri hill fort?
   a) Tipu Sultan
   b) Shivaji
   c) Aurangzeb
   d) Babur
4. Whose birth anniversary does the UN celebrate as International Day of Non-Violence?
   a) Mahatma Gandhi
   b) Adolf Hitler
   c) Indira Gandhi
   d) Amitabh Bachchan
5. Which famous diamond was stolen by Nadir Shah?
   a) Cullinan
   b) Koh-i-Noor
   c) Hope
   d) Ashoka

6. Who among the following was *not* a part of the conspiracy to assassinate Julius Caesar?
   a) Cassius
   b) Mark Antony
   c) Brutus
   d) Casca
7. Which of the following hill stations was formerly part of the kingdom of Sikkim?
   a) Ooty
   b) Darjeeling
   c) Nainital
   d) Shimla
8. In which of these places were two important battles fought by the Mughals?
   a) Benaras
   b) Kalinga
   c) Panipat
   d) Patna
9. Of which empire was Brihadratha Maurya the last ruler?
   a) The Maratha Empire
   b) The Mongol Empire
   c) The Mughal Empire
   d) The Mauryan Empire
10. Which is the first monument from Rajasthan to appear on the list of UNESCO World Heritage sites?
    a) Birla Planetarium
    b) Vijay Stambha
    c) Taj Mahal
    d) Jantar Mantar
11. In 1864, which city did John Lawrence make the

summer capital of British India?

a) Srinagar
b) Shimla
c) Kolkata
d) Mumbai

12. The foundation of which of the following landmarks did the fifth Sikh guru, Arjan Sahib, lay?

a) Lotus Temple
b) Golden Temple
c) Meenakshi Temple
d) Sun Temple

13. What kind of a tree is the Bo (Bodhi) tree?

a) Coconut
b) Mango
c) Peepal
d) Neem

14. In 1869, Frīdīric Auguste Bartholdi designed a statue of a woman with a torch named 'Egypt Brings Light to Asia' as a lighthouse for the Suez Canal. After this project failed, which famous structure did he complete in 1886?

a) Eiffel Tower
b) Statue of Liberty
c) Leaning Tower of Pisa
d) Pietm

15. To which famous king was Chanakya the chief adviser?

a) Chandragupta Maurya
b) Akbar
c) Iltutmish
d) Rajendra Chola

16. In which building situated in Delhi are the Nalanda Suite and the Marble Hall?
    a) Red Fort
    b) Parliament House
    c) Qutb Minar
    d) Rashtrapati Bhavan
17. Who named more than seventy cities after himself, including one at the mouth of the Nile?
    a) Attila the Hun
    b) Napoleon
    c) Alexander the Great
    d) Julius Caesar
18. The police force of which country issued the world's first car number plates in 1893?
    a) USA
    b) Germany
    c) France
    d) Russia
19. What is the popular name of the caves locally known as Verul Leni in Maharashtra?
    a) Bhimbetka rock shelters
    b) Ellora Caves
    c) Elephanta Caves
    d) Ajanta Caves
20. Who among the following was a descendant of Timur and Genghis Khan?
    a) Sher Shah
    b) Babur
    c) Tipu Sultan
    d) Iltutmish
21. Which was the first foreign country to issue postage

stamps with Gandhiji's picture?
a) South Africa
b) The United States of America
c) The United Kingdom
d) France

22. Shah Jahan built the Taj Mahal; what did Hamida Banu Begum build?
a) Gol Gumbaz
b) Diwan-i-Khas
c) Victoria Memorial
d) Humayun's Tomb

23. Which great Maratha warrior set up a cabinet of eight ministers known as 'Ashtapradhan'?
a) Aurangzeb
b) Shivaji
c) Nadir Shah
d) Tantia Tope

24. In 326 B.C., to whom did Ambhi give troops in return for aid against Porus?
a) Alexander the Great
b) Napoleon
c) Mahmud of Ghazni
d) Tamerlane

25. In 2014, which was the most visited ticketed monument?
a) The Taj Mahal
b) The Eiffel Tower
c) The Statue of Liberty
d) The Leaning Tower of Pisa

HISTORY-II

1. Which of the following was *not* one of the navratnas in Akbar's court?
   a) Todar Mal
   b) Abu'l-Fazl ibn Mubarak
   c) Faizi
   d) Bairam Khan
2. Gandhiji wrote that we must learn to live and die like Socrates and referred to him as a great:
   a) Swadeshi
   b) Sangrami
   c) Satyagrahi
   d) Sadhu
3. Which Mughal ruler did Maharana Pratap face at Haldighati?
   a) Shah Jahan
   b) Aurangzeb
   c) Akbar
   d) Jahangir
4. The tomb of which of the following rulers is *not* situated in Delhi?
   a) Firoz Shah Tughlaq
   b) Sikander Lodi
   c) Humayun
   d) Tipu Sultan
5. Which North Indian city is the birthplace of three Indian prime ministers?
   a) Allahabad

    b) Jammu

    c) Jaipur

    d) Bhatinda

6. Rani ki Vav, literally meaning 'the Queen's Stepwell', was recently added to the list of UNESCO World Heritage sites. In which state of India is it?

    a) Gujarat

    b) Madhya Pradesh

    c) Maharashtra

    d) Rajasthan

7. Which monument did Edouard de Laboulaye propose?

    a) Statue of Liberty

    b) Eiffel Tower

    c) Sydney Opera House

    d) Golden Gate Bridge

8. In 1915, to whom did the British award the Kaisar-i-Hind Gold Medal for his contribution to ambulance services in South Africa?

    a) Subhas Chandra Bose

    b) Jawaharlal Nehru

    c) Mahatma Gandhi

    d) Vallabhbhai Patel

9. What was the full name of the Mughal emperor born in 1592: Shahab-ud-din Muhammad _______?

    a) Humayun

    b) Akbar

    c) Jahangir

    d) Shah Jahan

10. At the foot of which monument is the memorial Amar Jawan Jyoti situated?

    a) Gateway of India
    b) India Gate
    c) Shahid Minar
    d) Red Fort

11. Which building designed by the British architect Edwin Lutyens is located at Raisina Hill in New Delhi?
    a) Lotus Temple
    b) Teen Murti Bhavan
    c) Rashtrapati Bhavan
    d) India Gate

12. The name of which historical movement in India literally means 'gift of land'?
    a) Appiko
    b) Bhoodan
    c) Chipko
    d) Navdanya

13. Among the following, who was named after the Italian city of her birth?
    a) Anjezn Gonxhe Bojaxhiu
    b) Florence Nightingale
    c) Marie Curie
    d) Margaret Elizabeth Noble

14. Who assumed the twin titles of Führer and Chancellor of Germany after Paul von Hindenburg's death?
    a) Winston Churchill
    b) Adolf Hitler
    c) Abraham Lincoln
    d) Benito Mussolini

15. Which structure did Guy de Maupassant ridicule as a 'high and skinny pyramid of iron ladders'?

a) Statue of Liberty
b) Leaning Tower of Pisa
c) Eiffel Tower
d) Sphinx

16. Which of the following monuments is the mausoleum of Muhammad Adil Shah?
a) Gol Gumbaz
b) Taj Mahal
c) Qutb Minar
d) Mohalla Bulbuli Khana

17. Of what did Mahatma Gandhi once send an autographed copy to Henry Ford?
a) An English translation of the Bhagavad Gita
b) A charkha
c) A khadi shawl
d) His walking stick

18. What did Maharaja Sawai Jai Singh II of Amber (later known as Jaipur) build in Delhi, Jaipur, Ujjain, Varanasi and Mathura?
a) Hawa Mahal
b) Jantar Mantar
c) Amer Fort
d) Neemrana Fort

19. Of which country is Hellenic Republic the official full name?
a) Hungary
b) Spain
c) Italy
d) Greece

20. Who spent his last 144 days in Birla House (now known as Gandhi Smriti), at No. 5, Tees January

Marg, New Delhi?
a) Mahatma Gandhi
b) Jawaharlal Nehru
c) Swami Vivekananda
d) Vallabhbhai Patel

21. Which was the eighth month of the early Roman republican calendar?
a) September
b) October
c) November
d) December

22. Whose tomb lies at a distance of two kilometres west of Haldighati?
a) Chetak
b) Bucephalus
c) Humayun
d) Shivaji

23. Beside which monument would you find the famous Quwwat-ul-Islam Mosque?
a) Buland Darwaza
b) Qutb Minar
c) Humayun's Tomb
d) Charminar

24. Which city did Emperor Akbar found under the name of Illahabas (blessed by God) in AD 1575, in Uttar Pradesh?
a) Fatehpur Sikri
b) Agra
c) Allahabad
d) Lucknow

25. Of which famous Mughal king was Princess Manmati
the mother?
a) Shah Jahan
b) Aurangzeb
c) Humayun
d) Babur

Please go sequentially from left to right (not following BODMAS)

You can add, subtract, multiply or divide to figure out the correct answer:

1	62		46		6		8	=	12
2	14		7		26		14	=	86
3	27		3		54		42	=	21
4	23		7		75		11	=	97
5	46		14		2		6	=	70
6	84		48		10		23	=	2
7	47		10		29		4	=	7
8	25		4		25		68	=	57

SPORTS

1. Till 2016, who was the oldest Indian to score an ODI hundred?
   a) Anil Kumble
   b) Sachin Tendulkar
   c) Sunil Gavaskar
   d) Kapil Dev
2. What signal does a cricket umpire give when he crosses his wrists below his waist?
   a) Dead ball
   b) Six
   c) One run short
   d) Wide
3. Which sporting event would you associate with a distance of 42.19 kilometres?
   a) Marathon
   b) Tour de France
   c) Formula One racing
   d) Relay race
4. For playing which of the following sports are elbow pads, hand pegs and touch pads required?
   a) Arm wrestling
   b) Shot put
   c) Kabaddi
   d) Boxing
5. Which of the following teams has played the least number of Test matches?
   a) Australia

   b) Zimbabwe
   c) India
   d) Pakistan
6. Who is the first Indian woman player to win a Grand Slam tennis tournament?
   a) Nirupama Sanjeev
   b) Shikha Uberoi
   c) Nirupama Mankad
   d) Sania Mirza
7. How many types of coloured cards can be shown in a game of field hockey?
   a) 6
   b) 4
   c) 3
   d) 2
8. Which of the following was introduced at the 1920 Antwerp Olympic Games?
   a) Mascot
   b) The Olympic flag with five rings
   c) Torch relay
   d) Gold medals
9. Who was the first batsman to score 400 runs in each of the first seven editions of the IPL?
   a) Suresh Raina
   b) Michael Hussey
   c) M.S. Dhoni
   d) Adam Gilchrist
10. In the inaugural edition of ISL (Indian Super League), which was the only other state, apart from Goa, to feature in the name of a team?
   a) Kerala

   b) Maharashtra
   c) Karnataka
   d) Gujarat

11. Who wrote the book titled *The Jubilee Book of Cricket*?
   a) Ranjitsinhji
   b) Duleepsinhji
   c) C.K. Nayudu
   d) I.A.K. Pataudi

12. Who among the following is the fastest to have scored 6,000 ODI runs?
   a) Rohit Sharma
   b) Suresh Raina
   c) Virat Kohli
   d) M.S. Dhoni

13. Till 2016, which team has played the largest number of IPL finals?
   a) Chennai Super Kings
   b) Mumbai Indians
   c) Kolkata Knight Riders
   d) Kings XI Punjab

14. Who holds the record for the biggest number of dismissals as a wicketkeeper in Test cricket?
   a) Adam Gilchrist
   b) Ian Healy
   c) M.S. Dhoni
   d) Mark Boucher

15. At the London Olympics of 1908, for which event was the distance from Windsor Castle to the Royal Box in the Olympic Stadium fixed?
   a) Triathlon

    b) Marathon
    c) Sailing
    d) Dressage

16. The father of which of these cricketers has played ODIs for India?
    a) M.S. Dhoni
    b) Yuvraj Singh
    c) Virender Sehwag
    d) Sachin Tendulkar

17. In which sport is the black rubber disc puck used?
    a) Sepak Takraw
    b) Volleyball
    c) Lacrosse
    d) Ice hockey

18. Name the Olympic sport in which the contest lasts for five minutes and takes place on a mat called 'tatami'.
    a) Karate
    b) Taekwondo
    c) Judo
    d) Sumo

19. Combining Tests, ODIs and T20s internationals, which cricketer has made the most hundreds in his career?
    a) Ricky Ponting
    b) Jacques Kallis
    c) Sachin Tendulkar
    d) Brian Lara

20. Imran Tahir and Usman Khawaja were both born in Pakistan. Imran plays for South Africa. For which team does Usman play?
    a) Australia

b) South Africa
c) West Indies
d) New Zealand

21. Whose autobiography is titled *Playing To Win*?
a) Sania Mirza
b) P.T. Usha
c) Jhulan Goswami
d) Saina Nehwal

22. Which of the following cards is *not* shown during a hockey match?
a) Red card
b) Green card
c) Yellow card
d) Blue card

23. Which of the following is *not* included in the Olympic triathlon?
a) Swimming
b) Running
c) Cycling
d) Shooting

24. What is the 'shot' in the Olympic sport shot put?
a) Hammer
b) Javelin
c) Metal ring
d) Metal ball

25. In which of the following sports is the red card *not* shown?
a) Football
b) Hockey
c) Table tennis
d) Billiards

LITERATURE-I

1. Which superhero was born in Forest Hills, Queens, New York?
   a) Phantom
   b) Spider-Man
   c) Superman
   d) Captain Vyom
2. Which novel by R.L. Stevenson was first published serially in a children's magazine under the title *The Sea Cook*?
   a) *Robinson Crusoe*
   b) *Ivanhoe*
   c) *Gulliver's Travels*
   d) *Treasure Island*
3. In which religion are the 547 stories of the *Jatakas* a part of the scriptures?
   a) Jainism
   b) Buddhism
   c) Judaism
   d) Islam
4. In *One Thousand and One Nights*, who uses the words, 'Open Sesame'?
   a) Sindbad
   b) Aladdin
   c) Ali Baba
   d) Gulliver
5. In Shakespeare's *The Merchant of Venice*, if Antonio failed to repay his loan to Shylock, he would have to give:

    a) A dozen diamonds
    b) A pound of his flesh
    c) His house
    d) His favourite horse

6. In the Harry Potter series, what is the fastest broomstick called?
    a) Firenze
    b) Flobberworm
    c) Nimbus
    d) Firebolt

7. In the novel *Animal Farm*, what kind of an animal was Napoleon?
    a. Pig
    b. Sheep
    c. Horse
    d. Kangaroo

8. In the Chacha Chaudhary comics, every time Sabu loses his temper, a volcano erupts on:
    a) Jupiter
    b) Saturn
    c) Earth
    d) Venus

9. In which imaginary town was the novel *Swami and Friends* by R.K. Narayan set?
    a. Timbuctoo
    b. Malgudi
    c. Wessex
    d. Dholakpur

10. In which present-day city was Rudyard Kipling born?
    a) Mumbai
    b) Kolkata

    c) Hyderabad

    d) New Delhi

11. Which of the following films is loosely based on Chetan Bhagat's book *Five Point Someone: What Not To Do at IIT*?

    a) *Munna Bhai M.B.B.S.*

    b) *3 Idiots*

    c) *Patiala House*

    d) *Lagaan*

12. Among the following, who was famous for writing dohas?

    a) Kabir

    b) Aryabhatta

    c) Ashoka

    d) Tenali Raman

13. Which superhero was born when Victor Stone met with an accident and his scientist-father saved him by replacing more than half his body with cybernetic parts?

    a) Cyborg

    b) Iron Man

    c) Hulk

    d) Wolverine

14. Which of the following is *not* the title of an autobiography?

    a) *Wings of Fire*

    b) *Long Walk to Freedom*

    c) *The Diary of a Young Girl*

    d) *A Brief History of Time*

15. Which Sanskrit work did the Asiatic Society first choose for English translation?

a) Mahabharata
b) Ramayana
c) *Abhijñānashākuntala*
d) *Jātaka Tales*

16. Which superhero gets his superpowers when he is caught in a gamma bomb explosion while trying to save a teenager's life?
a) Thor
b) Hulk
c) Iron Man
d) Captain America

17. Which language is also known in some areas as 'Gorkha Bhasa'?
a) Konkani
b) Nepali
c) Manipuri
d) Maithili

18. The name of which legendary prince of Denmark, the hero of a Shakespearean play, also means a small village?
a) Romeo
b) Hamlet
c) Macbeth
d) Henry

19. In comics, whose body was enhanced by the modified techno-organic virus Extremis?
a) Superman
b) Spider-Man
c) Batman
d) Iron Man

20. Which of the following was named the 'New Oxford

American Dictionary's 2009 Word of the Year'?
a) Unfriend
b) Tweet
c) Selfie
d) Phablet

21. In *Alice's Adventures in Wonderland,* who is the only character with whom Alice interacts outside of Wonderland?
a) The Mad Hatter
b) Alice's sister
c) The Queen of Hearts
d) The Rabbit

22. Which comic-strip character has a brain that works faster than a computer?
a) Chacha Chaudhary
b) Suppandi
c) Pavitr Prabhakar
d) Shaktimaan

23. In which novel would you meet characters named Jim Hawkins and Billy Bones?
a) *Oliver Twist*
b) *Treasure Island*
c) *Robinson Crusoe*
d) *Ivanhoe*

24. Hero is the Phantom's horse; what species of animal is Devil?
a) Lion
b) Wolf
c) Camel
d) Cheetah

25. Which famous author is credited with introducing expressions like 'fasionable', 'foregone conclusion' and 'wild goose chase'?
    a) Lewis Carroll
    b) Thomas Hardy
    c) Charles Dickens
    d) William Shakespeare

FUN FACTS-4

1. Nairobi, the capital of Kenya, means 'cool water' in the Maasai language.
2. The chemical element Polonium is named after Poland, the birthplace of its discoverer, Marie Curie.
3. J.R.R. Tolkien, the author of *The Lord of the Rings* books, had a deep interest in languages. He invented several languages, such as Elvish, Dwarvish, Entish, and Black Speech.
4. Your heart beats 1,00,000 times per day, pumping 5.5 litres per minute. This will add up to about 3 million litres of blood a year.
5. About 28,000 kg of strawberries and 7,000 litres of cream are consumed at the Wimbledon tournament each year.
6. The X-Ray was accidentally discovered by Wilhelm Roentgen, Professor of Physics in Worzburg, Bavaria, while he was experimenting with cathode rays. The first-ever X-ray image was that of his wife's hand.
7. Pizza Margherita is commonly believed to have been named in honour of Queen of Italy, Margherita of Savoy, and of the unification of Italy: the toppings are tomato (red), mozzarella (white) and basil (green), representing the colours of the flag of Italy.
8. Mount Everest was previously known as Peak XV. It was renamed in honour of the British Surveyor General of India, Sir George Everest.

9. In 2015, for the first time, the Oxford Dictionaries Word of the Year was not a word. It was a pictograph, the 'Face with Tears of Joy' emoji.

10. Grammy winner Lorde was born as Ella Marija Lani Yelich-O'Connor in New Zealand.

11. The names of seventy-two French scientists, engineers and mathematicians were engraved by Gustave Eiffel on the four sides of the Eiffel Tower under the first balcony, because of his concern over the protests against the tower.

12. The tongue of a blue whale weighs as much as an elephant. Also, a blue whale has the slowest heartbeat of any animal, beating just four to eight times a minute.

1. Who was made a prisoner on the island of Lilliput?
   a) Alice
   b) Swami
   c) Gulliver
   d) Robin Hood
2. Which work revolves around the life of Philip Pirrip?
   a) *Nicholas Nickleby*
   b) *Great Expectations*
   c) *The Old Curiosity Shop*
   d) *Pickwick Papers*
3. What is the name of the talking monkey in *Chhota Bheem*?
   a) Kalia
   b) Raju
   c) Chutki
   d) Jaggu
4. Which of the following was known in Europe as *The Fables of Bidpai*?
   a) *Panchatantra*
   b) Bhagavad Gita
   c) *One Thousand and One Nights*
   d) Mahabharata
5. Which term comes from a medieval Latin word meaning 'manual or book of words'?
   a) Calendar
   b) Dictionary

    c) Atlas

    d) Directory

6. In the first sketches of which superhero did the artist, Bob Kane, give him wings and red tights?

    a) Spider-Man

    b) Superman

    c) Batman

    d) Shaktimaan

7. Who eats a cake marked 'Eat Me', which causes her to grow very tall?

    a) Alice

    b) Thumbelina

    c) Rapunzel

    d) The Cheshire Cat

8. In the Harry Potter series of books, what kind of a place is Azkaban?

    a) A prison

    b) A bank

    c) A school

    d) A wand shop

9. In the world of comics, what is the name of Tintin's dog?

    a) Tommy

    b) Spike

    c) Snowy

    d) Scobby

10. In the Tom and Jerry cartoons, what kind of a creature is Spike?

    a) Cat

    b) Dog

c) Fox
d) Wolf

11. Who designed the cover for the Bengali translation of Jim Corbett's *Man-Eaters of Kumaon* and the first edition of Jawaharlal Nehru's *The Discovery of India*?
    a) Rabindranath Tagore
    b) Ravi Shankar
    c) R.K. Laxman
    d) Satyajit Ray

12. About which famous author did Leo Tolstoy write: 'I remember the astonishment I felt when I first read _________. ... not only did I feel no delight, but I felt an irresistible repulsion and tedium...'?
    a) Karl Marx
    b) William Shakespeare
    c) Rudyard Kipling
    d) Charles Dickens

13. Which comic-strip character lives in Bengalla?
    a) Batman
    b) Superman
    c) The Phantom
    d) Shaktiman

14. Which famous novel begins with the line: 'It was the best of times, it was the worst of times...'?
    a) *War and Peace*
    b) *Alice's Adventures in Wonderland*
    c) *The Adventures of Huckleberry Finn*
    d) *A Tale of Two Cities*

15. Which book was translated into Arabic as *Kalila Wa-Dimna*?
    a) *Pride and Prejudice*

    b) *Panchatantra*

    c) *Gita Govinda*

    d) *Arthashastra*

16. In Asterix comics, who could make beautiful flowers grow in moments?

    a) Getafix

    b) Botanix

    c) Prefix

    d) Suffix

17. In English, which of the following punctuation marks is symbolized by two dots?

    a) Semicolon

    b) Comma

    c) Exclamation mark

    d) Colon

18. What do you call a word, a name or a phrase that is formed by rearranging the letters of another word, name or phrase?

    a) Oxymoron

    b) Simile

    c) Anagram

    d) Metaphor

19. With which comic-strip character would you associate Gwen Stacy?

    a) Spider-Man

    b) Superman

    c) Batman

    d) The Phantom

20. Which of the following words is derived from the Latin word meaning 'more'?

    a) Plus

    b) Minus
    c) Cos
    d) Pi

21. In 1937, Crystal City in Texas erected a statue to honor E.C. Segar and Popeye for their:
    a) Positive influence on America's eating habits
    b) Contribution to environment awareness
    c) Role in developing reading habits
    d) Role in developing sleeping habits

22. Whose autobiography is titled *Autobiography: The Story of My Experiments with Truth*?
    a) Mahatma Gandhi
    b) Jawaharlal Nehru
    c) Swami Vivekananda
    d) Vallabhbhai Patel

23. Morty and Ferdie are the nephews of a famous cartoon character. Who is he?
    a) Popeye
    b) Donald Duck
    c) Henry
    d) Mickey Mouse

24. According to Jules Verne's novel *The Moon-Voyage*, which 'valuable metal possesses the whiteness of silver, the indestructibility of gold, the tenacity of iron, the fusibility of copper, the lightness of glass'?
    a) Platinum
    b) Aluminium
    c) Tin
    d) Lead

25. Which of the following superheroes gets his powers from a ring?

a) Superman
b) The Phantom
c) Batman
d) Green Lantern

ENTERTAINMENT

1. The wax statue of Kareena Kapoor in Madame Tussauds' was restyled in an outfit from which of her films?
   a) *Kabhi Khushi Kabhie Gham*
   b) *Omkara*
   c) *Jab We Met*
   d) *Ra.One*

2. Which maestro taught George Harrison to play the sitar?
   a) Sultan Vilayat Khan
   b) Allauddin Khan
   c) Ravi Shankar
   d) Zakir Hussain

3. In which film did Nirupa Roy say, '*Tu abhi itna ameer nahi hua, beta, ki apni maa ko kharid sake*'?
   a) *Sholay*
   b) *Zanjeer*
   c) *Silsila*
   d) *Deewar*

4. Which actor's screen name has been Vijay in more than twenty Hindi films?
   a) Rishi Kapoor
   b) Amitabh Bachchan
   c) Dharmendra
   d) Hrithik Roshan

5. Who was the director of the 2014 film *PK*?
   a) Aamir Khan

    b) Rajkumar Hirani
    c) Prabhu Deva
    d) Dibakar Banerjee

6. On Google, who was the most-searched Bollywood male actor in 2014?
    a) Shah Rukh Khan
    b) Ranbir Kapoor
    c) Akshay Kumar
    d) Salman Khan

7. The 2007 film *Guru* is loosely based on the life of:
    a) Shah Rukh Khan
    b) Dhirubhai Ambani
    c) Rabindranath Tagore
    d) Dilip Kumar

8. In 1946, who designed the cover for Jawaharlal Nehru's book *Discovery of India*?
    a) Bimal Roy
    b) Satyajit Ray
    c) Mrinal Sen
    d) Guru Dutt

9. Which famous Hindi film actor is the grandson of the well-known Urdu poet Harivansh Rai Srivastava?
    a) Amitabh Bachchan
    b) Shah Rukh Khan
    c) Saif Ali Khan
    d) Abhishek Bachchan

10. Who played the female lead in the films *Delhi-6*, *Aisha* and *Saawariya*?
    a) Sonam Kapoor
    b) Deepika Padukone
    c) Priyanka Chopra

    d) Amrita Rao

11. Who played the role of Milkha Singh in the film, *Bhaag Milkha Bhaag*?
    a) Ranbir Kapoor
    b) Farhan Akhtar
    c) Hrithik Roshan
    d) Arjun Kapoor

12. The father of which of the following film directors founded Dharma Productions?
    a) Sanjay Leela Bhansali
    b) Aditya Chopra
    c) Karan Johar
    d) Farhan Akhtar

13. What is the name of the witch in the film *Chhota Bheem and the Throne of Bali*?
    a) Indumati
    b) Rangda
    c) Tuntun
    d) Meena

14. Who is the famous husband of actress Genelia D'Souza?
    a) Saif Ali Khan
    b) Riteish Deshmukh
    c) Imran Khan
    d) Ranveer Singh

15. In which animated film series would you come across a mammoth named Manny, a sabre-toothed tiger named Diego, and a sloth named Sid?
    a) *Ice Age*
    b) *Shrek*
    c) *The Lion King*

    d) *Madagascar*

16. With which film did Karan Johar make his directorial debut?
    a) *Kuch Kuch Hota Hai*
    b) *My Name Is Khan*
    c) *Dilwale Dulhania Le Jayenge*
    d) *Student of the Year*

17. In the Harry Potter films, which of the following characters has been played by Ralph Fiennes, Christian Coulson and Richard Bremmer?
    a) Lord Voldemort
    b) Vernon Dursley
    c) Albus Dumbledore
    d) Nicolas Flamel

18. For which popular film did Kirron Kher suggest the title?
    a) *Dilwale Dulhania Le Jayenge*
    b) *Ra.One*
    c) *Taare Zameen Par*
    d) *Kai Po Che!*

19. Who played the role of Imraan in the 2011 film *Zindagi Na Milegi Dobara*?
    a) Farhan Akhtar
    b) Hrithik Roshan
    c) Abhay Deol
    d) Saif Ali Khan

20. Which film series has the characters Woody and Buzz Lightyear?
    a) *Toy Story*
    b) *Shrek*
    c) *The Lion King*

    d) *Ice Age*

21. Which of the following films did *not* feature a real-life father and son as father and son?
    a) *Yamla Pagla Deewana*
    b) *Sarkar*
    c) *Munna Bhai M.B.B.S.*
    d) *Bunty Aur Babli*

22. Who provided the voice for the monkey in the film *Kung Fu Panda*?
    a) Brad Pitt
    b) Tom Cruise
    c) Dustin Hoffman
    d) Jackie Chan

23. Who was the director of the 2014 film *Happy New Year*?
    a) Sujoy Ghosh
    b) Vishal Bhardwaj
    c) Anurag Kashyap
    d) Farah Khan

24. Who is the well-knowns son of actress Neetu Singh?
    a) Ranbir Kapoor
    b) Arjun Kapoor
    c) Shahid Kapur
    d) Varun Dhawan

25. Among the following actors, who has represented India in rugby for almost twenty-five years?
    a) Aamir Khan
    b) Rahul Bose
    c) Farhan Akhtar
    d) Abhishek Bachchan

SCIENCE AND TECHNOLOGY-I

1. Which of the following planets is *not* named after Greek or Roman gods and goddesses?
   a) Mars
   b) Uranus
   c) Venus
   d) Earth
2. With which of the following applications is the phrase 'Last seen' most commonly associated?
   a) YouTube
   b) WhatsApp
   c) Instagram
   d) Twitter
3. With which planet of the solar system would you associate the Cassini Division?
   a) Uranus
   b) Saturn
   c) Neptune
   d) Jupiter
4. What connects Belka, Strelka and Laika? They are:
   a) Dogs in space
   b) Russian folk dances
   c) Russian sweets
   d) Russian hats
5. What did the first webcam in the world show?
   a) Coffee pot
   b) Computer
   c) Traffic jam
   d) Apple

6. The name of which instrument comes from two Greek words meaning 'chest' and 'to explore'?
   a) Stethoscope
   b) Barometer
   c) Thermometer
   d) Pacemaker
7. On Facebook, you have the option of changing your language to which of the following?
   a) English (Mafia)
   b) English (Daredevil)
   c) English (Pirate)
   d) English (Hoodlum)
8. Since its discovery in September 1846, which planet completed its first revolution of the sun in 2011?
   a) Mars
   b) Titan
   c) Earth
   d) Neptune
9. Who is credited with the invention of television?
   a) John Logie Baird
   b) Thomas Edison
   c) Nikola Tesla
   d) Johannes Gutenberg
10. Humphry Davy researched a 'substance X', whose properties were similar to those of chlorine. What was 'substance X' later known as?
    a) Bromine
    b) Iodine
    c) Carbon
    d) Oxygen
11. While working with Windows, which key should you

press along with the Ctrl key to close a spreadsheet?
a) W
b) O
c) S
d) C

12. Who invented the magnetic credit card strip in 1968?
a) Eli Whitney
b) Samuel O'Reilly
c) Ron Klein
d) Rudolf Diesel

13. The process of converting information or data into a code, especially to prevent unauthorized access, is known as:
a) Encryption
b) Reboot
c) Zipfile
d) Spam

14. Robert Cornelius, an amateur chemist and photpgraphy enthusiast, in 1839, is believed to be credited with the world's first:
a) Instant message
b) Tweet
c) Selfie
d) Blog

15. If the oxygen supply is high, the colour of a flame appears:
a) Blue
b) Yellow
c) Red
d) Green

16. Which famous Indian's first book was titled *Molecular*

Diffraction of Light?
a) A.P.J. Abdul Kalam
b) C.V. Raman
c) Har Gobind Khorana
d) Vikram Sarabhai

17. Which video game has characters like Scarlett Fox and Montana Smith?
a) Candy Crush Saga
b) Temple Run
c) Subway Surfers
d) Fruit Ninja

18. In an SLR camera, if 'S' stands for 'single' and 'L' stands for 'lens', what does 'R' stand for?
a) Record
b) Reprography
c) Reflex
d) Rotation

19. What is a unit of information equal to 1,048,576 bytes called?
a) Gigabyte
b) Megabyte
c) Terabyte
d) Kilobyte

20. What did Sir Percy Spencer invent following the accidental melting of a candy bar?
a) Pressure cooker
b) Microwave oven
c) Refrigerator
d) Vacuum cleaner

21. While working on Windows, which key should you press along with the 'Alt' key to close the current

window?
a) F1
b) F2
c) F3
d) F4

22. On a standard computer keyboard, what do the four keys arranged in an inverted T formation have on them?
a) Arrows
b) Dots
c) Question marks
d) Comma

23. Which of the following words comes from two Greek words meaning 'alongside' and 'food'?
a) Virus
b) Bacteria
c) Parasite
d) Protein

24. Which symbol did Chris Messina, a former designer at Google, propose for Twitter that was earlier known as the 'pound symbol'?
a) Double ticks
b) Hashtag
c) At sign
d) Like

25. Who is credited with being the first person to look at the moon through a telescope?
a) Christopher Columbus
b) Galileo Galilei
c) Alexander Graham Bell
d) Stephen Hawking

MATHS-IV

Please go sequentially from left to right (not following BODMAS)

You can add, subtract, multiply or divide to figure out the correct answer:

1	19		5		26		3	=	23
2	18		9		36		47	=	25
3	13		7		31		3	=	20
4	58		12		34		16	=	5
5	15		7		75		26	=	56
6	42		16		2		3	=	87
7	36		18		3		35	=	89
8	26		44		35		7	=	5

SCIENCE AND TECHNOLOGY-II

1. Argentina is named after the Latin name of which metal?
   a) Silver
   b) Copper
   c) Iron
   d) Helium
2. With the help of which natural phenomenon was Albert Einstein's 'General Theory of Relativity' proved?
   a) Rainbow
   b) Total solar eclipse
   c) Mirage
   d) Tsunami
3. Till 2016, which language was used by the biggest number of internet users?
   a) Hindi
   b) English
   c) Spanish
   d) Japanese
4. Which discovery is regarded by scientists as the 'greatest event in chemistry since the discovery of oxygen'?
   a) Radium
   b) X-rays
   c) Raman rays
   d) Laughing gas
5. Who amongst the following was the nephew of Sir C.V. Raman?

   a) Har Gobind Khorana
   b) S. Chandrasekhar
   c) Homi Bhabha
   d) Jagadish Chandra Bose
6. Which of the following is an output device for a computer?
   a) Joystick
   b) Mouse
   c) Keyboard
   d) LCD
7. Which metal, among all metals, has the highest known electrical and thermal conductivity?
   a) Gold
   b) Silver
   c) Platinum
   d) Aluminium
8. Who among the following coined the term radioactivity?
   a) Marie Curie
   b) Henri Becquerel
   c) Alfred Nobel
   d) Ernest Rutherford
9. Till 2016, which country had the largest number of mobile phone users?
   a) India
   b) Mozambique
   c) Brazil
   d) China
10. Which is the windiest planet in the solar system and takes 165 earth years to revolve around the sun?
   a) Uranus

b) Saturn
c) Neptune
d) Jupiter

11. To which animal did the Americans refer as Muttnik?
a) Dolly
b) Black Beauty
c) Laika
d) Elsa

12. Which of the following is an operating system?
a) Binary
b) Microsoft
c) C++
d) Linux

13. In which category did both Marie Curie and her daughter, Irène Curie, win the Nobel Prize?
a) Medicine
b) Literature
c) Peace
d) Chemistry

14. Who was inspired by the blue colour of the Mediterranean Sea to develop his Nobel Prize-winning theory?
a) C.V. Raman
b) Isaac Newton
c) Albert Einstein
d) Thomas Alva Edison

15. Which of the following combinations is used to save a document in MS Word?
a) Ctrl + F
b) Ctrl + S
c) Ctrl + Alt

    d) Ctrl + Del

16. Which was the most distant planet in our solar system before Pluto was discovered in 1930?
    a) Jupiter
    b) Saturn
    c) Mercury
    d) Neptune

17. The heaviest of all planets rotates faster than any other planet. Name it.
    a) Jupiter
    b) Venus
    c) Mercury
    d) Neptune

18. In 1963, Douglas Engelbart invented and developed the first working model. Twenty years later, what was mass produced using his idea?
    a) Mobile phone
    b) Computer mouse
    c) Iced tea
    d) Computer keyboard

19. In 1896, who gave up German citizenship and was not a citizen of any country until 1901?
    a) Adolf Hitler
    b) Karl Marx
    c) Albert Einstein
    d) V. Lenin

20. Which of the following melts at around 1064°C and boils at around -2856°C?
    a) Cadmium
    b) Gold
    c) Helium

    d) Mercury

21. In 1923, Frederick G. Banting and John Macleod received the Nobel Prize in Physiology or Medicine for the discovery of:
    a) Insulin
    b) Penicillin
    c) Smallpox vaccine
    d) Blood groups

22. The element with the chemical symbol 'Es' is named after:
    a) Albert Einstein
    b) Thomas Alva Edison
    c) Ernest Rutherford
    d) Ernest Hemingway

23. Of which country is .es the internet code?
    a) India
    b) Spain
    c) Ethiopia
    d) Ecuador

24. Which of the following chemical elements is named after an inventor?
    a) Californium
    b) Uranium
    c) Nobelium
    d) Gold

25. Liberty, Equality and Fraternity are the arcs of a ring of this planet:
    a) Mercury
    b) Venus
    c) Neptune
    d) Saturn

GEOGRAPHY-I

1. In Japan, *goraiko* is a special name for:
   a) The sunrise seen from Mount Fuji
   b) The tea used in a tea ceremony
   c) The longest river
   d) The best samurai
2. In which state of India is the city of Tezpur?
   a) Bihar
   b) Assam
   c) Chhattisgarh
   d) Odisha
3. A line on a map joining points of equal height, above or below sea level, is called:
   a) Contour line
   b) Isohyet
   c) Latitude
   d) Isobar
4. Which continent has been inhabited for the longest period of time?
   a) Africa
   b) Antarctica
   c) Uzbekistan
   d) Australia
5. In which country is the UNESCO World Heritage Site Aapravasi Ghat situated?
   a) Fiji
   b) Mauritius
   c) Sri Lanka

    d) China

6. Which continent is classified as a desert?
   a) Asia
   b) Antarctica
   c) Europe
   d) North America

7. In which present-day country would you see the archaeological ruins of Mohenjo-daro?
   a) Pakistan
   b) Sri Lanka
   c) Bhutan
   d) Nepal

8. What is the island Más a Tierra, on which Alexander Selkirk was marooned, now officially known as?
   a) West Indies
   b) Robinson Crusoe Island
   c) Mauritius
   d) Gulliver Island

9. Apart from India, with which country does Bangladesh share its land boundaries?
   a) Myanmar
   b) Pakistan
   c) China
   d) Russia

10. Which is the largest country in the world with a single time zone?
   a) Sri Lanka
   b) China
   c) Brazil
   d) USA

11. An extensive group of islands is called an:

    a) Archipelago
    b) Aggradation
    c) Atoll
    d) Anticline

12. In which state of India do the districts of Korea and Bastar fall?
    a) Chhattisgarh
    b) Jharkhand
    c) Madhya Pradesh
    d) Kerala

13. Which is the largest westward-flowing river of India?
    a) Narmada
    b) Ganga
    c) Irrawaddy
    d) Godavari

14. On an atlas, like which letter would Vietnam be shaped?
    a) V
    b) S
    c) T
    d) X

15. Which continent has the longest coastline?
    a) Australia
    b) Africa
    c) Europe
    d) Asia

16. In which country is around 60 per cent of the Sunderbans forest found?
    a) Nepal
    b) Bangladesh
    c) Sri Lanka

    d) India

17. Which river is often called 'Old Ganga' or 'Dakshin Ganga'?
    a) Yamuna
    b) Godavari
    c) Brahmaputra
    d) Narmada

18. On which river in Assam is Mājuli, a freshwater river island, located?
    a) Ganges
    b) Krishna
    c) Brahmaputra
    d) Kaveri

19. Which is the warmest and saltiest sea in the world?
    a) Arctic Ocean
    b) Caspian Sea
    c) Arabian Sea
    d) Red Sea

20. Which of the following states is landlocked?
    a) Bihar
    b) Orissa
    c) Maharashtra
    d) Karnataka

21. After whom has a lake in the Alpenrausch in Switzerland been named?
    a) Rajesh Khanna
    b) Amitabh Bachchan
    c) Shah Rukh Khan
    d) Yash Chopra

22. Between India and which other country does the Palk Strait lie?

a) Bangladesh
b) Nepal
c) Pakistan
d) Sri Lanka

23. To which river did the Greeks refer as Zaradros?
    a) Chenab
    b) Ravi
    c) Beas
    d) Sutlej

24. Of which desert is the Mount Koussi summit the highest point?
    a) Sahara
    b) Namib
    c) Gobi
    d) Kalahari

25. Which river in India is often referred to as the 'Vridha Ganga' because of its length?
    a) Godavari
    b) Cauvery
    c) Krishna
    d) Luni

GEOGRAPHY-II

1. Which is the southernmost continent in the world?
   a) Antarctica
   b) Europe
   c) Australia
   d) Africa
2. Which of the following capital cities is situated in Asia?
   a) Cairo
   b) Jakarta
   c) Lima
   d) Amsterdam
3. Which of the following countries shares the shortest international boundary with India?
   a) Nepal
   b) China
   c) Myanmar
   d) Bhutan
4. With an altitude of 11,942 feet, which of the following is the highest administrative capital city in the world?
   a) La Paz
   b) Sydney
   c) Beijing
   d) Brasilia
5. Of which state in India is the Kathiawar Peninsula a part?
   a) Tamil Nadu
   b) Kerala

    c) Gujarat
    d) Madhya Pradesh

6. The name of which of the following clouds comes from the Latin word for 'heap'?
    a) Cirrus
    b) Nimbus
    c) Stratus
    d) Cumulus

7. Which is the smallest country in Asia in terms of size?
    a) Sri Lanka
    b) Bangladesh
    c) Singapore
    d) Maldives

8. After which freedom fighter is the road in Mumbai—originally and more popularly known as Marine Drive—named?
    a) Vallabhbhai Patel
    b) Jawaharlal Nehru
    c) Mahatma Gandhi
    d) Subhas Chandra Bose

9. On which continent is French Guiana, an overseas department and region of France, located?
    a) South America
    b) Europe
    c) Asia
    d) Africa

10. Which Indian union territory has around 572 islands of which only 37 are inhabited?
    a) Daman and Diu
    b) Lakshadweep
    c) Dadra and Nagar Haveli

    d) Andaman and Nicobar Islands

11. Princess Konohanasakuya-hime is worshipped as the supernatural deity of one of the following peaks. Which one is it?

    a) Kilimanjaro

    b) Mount Fuji

    c) Mount Aconcagua

    d) K2

12. Through which state does the Indus River enter India?

    a) Punjab

    b) Uttarakhand

    c) Jammu and Kashmir

    d) Rajasthan

13. In the desert, what is classified as crescentic, star, linear, dome and parabolic?

    a) Cacti

    b) Mirages

    c) Dunes

    d) Oases

14. In which state is the Rajaji National Park located?

    a) Assam

    b) Uttarakhand

    c) Madhya Pradesh

    d) Karnataka

15. Of which Asian nation is Luzon the largest island?

    a) Philippines

    b) Indonesia

    c) Malaysia

    d) Japan

16. Through which country neighbouring India do the

    Kelani Ganga and Kalu Ganga flow?
a) Nepal
b) Sri Lanka
c) Bangladesh
d) Cambodia

17. Which is the only continent without glaciers?
a) Australia
b) Antarctica
c) Europe
d) Africa

18. In which Indian state are the Vagator, Arambol and Morjim beaches located?
a) Maharashtra
b) Goa
c) Tamil Nadu
d) Kerala

19. Which city in Uttarakhand is also known as Mayapuri, Kapila and Gangadwar?
a) Almora
b) Haridwar
c) Dehra Dun
d) Chamoli

20. Which is the highest free-standing mountain in the world?
a) Mount Fuji
b) Mont Blanc
c) Mount Kilimanjaro
d) Mount Aconcagua

21. In which country would you get to see the 'Ten-Thousand-Li Wall'?
a) China

b) Afghanistan
c) Japan
d) Thailand

22. The first aerial survey of which peak was made in 1933?
a) Mount Everest
b) Mount Fuji
c) Mount Kilimanjaro
d) K2

23. Which is the largest city in Iraq?
a) Cairo
b) Baghdad
c) Mosul
d) Karbala

24. More than 70 km long, what is sometimes referred to as the 'white snake'?
a) The Ganges
b) Khyber Pass
c) The Siachen Glacier
d) Nilgiri mountains

25. In 1621, which geographical phenomenon did scientist Pierre Gassendi name after the Roman goddess of dawn and the Roman god of the north wind?
a) Aurora Australis
b) Aurora Borealis
c) Oasis
d) Mirage

FOOD

1. Which spice is known as 'meetha jeera' in Bengali?
   a) Celery
   b) Aniseed
   c) Fennel
   d) Cinnamon
2. The tomato was introduced to Europe by the:
   a) Germans
   b) Spanish
   c) French
   d) Greeks
3. Of which fruit are clementine and tangerine varieties?
   a) Apple
   b) Orange
   c) Guava
   d) Banana
4. The name of which vegetable comes from an Old French word meaning 'head'?
   a) Brinjal
   b) Cabbage
   c) Bottle gourd
   d) Pumpkin
5. The recipe for 'jahangiri', a sweet dish, is believed to be listed in al-Baghdadi's cookery book of the thirteenth century. By which name do we know it?
   a) Kulfi
   b) Jalebi
   c) Gulab Jamun

    d) Barfi

6. Kufri Chandramukhi, Kufri Jyoti, Kufri Badshah, Kufri Sindhuri, Kufri Lalima are the main varieties of what grown in India?
   a) Wheat
   b) Apple
   c) Potato
   d) Rice

7. Kakori kebab, a famous Awadhi recipe, gets its name from a town in:
   a) Andhra Pradesh
   b) West Bengal
   c) Uttar Pradesh
   d) Tamil Nadu

8. Which spice is called *opiumvallmo* in Swedish?
   a) Fennel
   b) Poppy seeds
   c) Pepper
   d) Oregano

9. Which of the following is a Parsi dish usually made of chicken or meat, vegetables and lentils?
   a) Litti
   b) Ghevar
   c) Dhansak
   d) Shahi Tukra

10. Traditionally, what is the main component of 'gatte' in the dish gatte ki sabzi?
   a) Besan
   b) Paneer
   c) Potato
   d) Rajma

11. Which of the following sweets is similar to a lalmohan?
    a) Jalebi
    b) Gulab Jamun
    c) Petha
    d) Rabri

12. Grown only at Alirajpur in Madhya Pradesh, of what is Noor Jahan a variety?
    a) Orange
    b) Apple
    c) Mango
    d) Grapes

13. Of which of the following is lasagna a variety?
    a) Pickle
    b) Pasta
    c) Salad
    d) Pizza

14. In which of the following places did the dish momo originate?
    a) Tibet
    b) South Korea
    c) Vietnam
    d) Jordan

15. Ranbir, Taraori, Kasturi and Mahi Sugandha are varieties of:
    a) Basmati rice
    b) Darjeeling tea
    c) Rasgullas
    d) Motichoor laddoos

16. Which spice is the dried unopened bud of *Syzygium aromaticum*?

    a) Cardamom
    b) Cinnamon
    c) Clove
    d) Nutmeg

17. Which grain is the staple food of about half of the world's population?
    a) Wheat
    b) Rice
    c) Bajra
    d) Jowar

18. What is the main ingredient of the dish upma?
    a) Semolina/rawa/suji
    b) Rice
    c) Chickpea flour/besan
    d) Corn

19. Which state is known for the dish litti-chokha?
    a) Bihar
    b) Maharashtra
    c) Kerala
    d) Tamil Nadu

20. Which spice is called 'zafran' in Urdu?
    a) Saffron
    b) Turmeric
    c) Ginger
    d) Garlic

21. Of which country neighbouring India is hilsa the national fish?
    a) Bangladesh
    b) Sri Lanka
    c) Nepal
    d) Pakistan

22. To which edible plant product did the Spanish explorers give a name meaning 'grinning face'?
    a) Coconut
    b) Watermelon
    c) Papaya
    d) Guava

23. What is Chhota Bheem's favourite sweet?
    a) Laddoo
    b) Barfi
    c) Jalebi
    d) Rasgulla

24. Which is the world's most imported fresh fruit in terms of volume?
    a) Banana
    b) Guava
    c) Apple
    d) Orange

25. Which fruit is supposed to have inspired Isaac Newton to propound his law of gravitation?
    a) Apple
    b) Orange
    c) Guava
    d) Strawberry

BUZZER ROUND

SET-1

1. In which century was the Nobel Peace Prize first awarded?
2. With which animal would you associate the Bikaner Festival in Rajasthan?
3. Who is the first Nobel-Laureate mother of a Nobel-Laureate daughter?
4. 'Jana Gana Mana' was officially adopted as India's national anthem in 1947: serious or joking?
5. Of which novel is 'Call me Ishmael' a famous first line?
6. Rajasthan is the largest state in India in terms of area; which is the second largest?
7. After which Roman general is the month of July named?
8. Who was the last governor-general to win the Bharat Ratna?
9. Which hockey player's birthday is celebrated as National Sports Day in India?
10. To whom did Akbar award the title of 'Miyan' at Fatehpur Sikri?

SET-2

1. The colour white is common to the flags of Bangladesh and India: serious or joking?
2. In which city of India is the Meenakshi Amman

Temple situated?

3. Which number does Amitabh Bachchan's first film have in its name?
4. Male platypuses are venomous: serious or joking?
5. In 1914, who was appointed director of The Kaiser Wilhelm Institute for Physics in Berlin?
6. Whom did Bahadur Shah I succeed as the Mughal emperor of India?
7. If you add the even numbers on a dice, how much would you get?
8. In *Swami and Friends*, Swami played for the MCC. What did 'M' in MCC stand for?
9. Which is the largest district in India?
10. Which tennis star's autobiography is titled *Open: An Autobiography*?

SET-3

1. Of which branch of the armed services is 'Shano Varuna' the motto?
2. Of which princely state of India was the ruler conventionally known as the Nizam?
3. Tapir is an underwater creature: serious or joking?
4. In which film did Aamir Khan play the role of a sepoy of the British East India Company?
5. Who is credited with inventing the hydraulic screw for raising water?
6. Your father's only sister's mother's only son is your ...
7. To which Indian document did 284 members append their signatures on 24 January 1950?
8. On the banks of which lake is the Nishat Bagh in Jammu and Kashmir located?

9. Whose autobiography is titled *The Diary of a Young Girl*?
10. Of which football club was Sir Alex Ferguson the manager for twenty-six years?

SET-4

1. Samurais are an ancient warrior caste of China: serious or joking?
2. Whose tomb, exacavated by Howard Carter, revealed around 5,398 objects?
3. Birds have small, sharp teeth: serious or joking?
4. Which actress made her Hindi film debut with the 2010 film *Dabangg*?
5. The name of which life-saving object means 'protection against fall' in French?
6. Alphabetically, the name of which colour of the rainbow would appear first in a dictionary?
7. The Bharat Ratna medal is shaped like the leaf of the neem tree: serious or joking?
8. In which category did Winston Churchill win the Nobel Prize in 1953?
9. Which country does Rafael Nadal represent in tennis?
10. In Windows, which key should you press along with the Ctrl key to select an entire document?

SET-5

1. In which country is the Jigme Singye Wangchuck National Park?
2. The best-preserved part of this UNESCO World Heritage Site dates to the Ming dynasty. Name it.
3. Jellyfish are fish: serious or joking?

4. In which country did the cartoon character Doraemon originate?
5. Pb is the symbol of which chemical element?
6. On whose golden jubilee in 1887 was the Chhatrapati Shivaji Terminus in Mumbai formally opened?
7. Which state is known as 'Srigandhada Nadu', meaning the 'the land of sandalwood'?
8. On the right bank of which river is the Taj Mahal situated?
9. Shakespeare is known as the Bard of Avon: serious or joking?
10. Which Grand Slam tournament is also referred to as Roland Garros?

SET-6

1. If you arrange the colours of the rainbow in alphabetical order, which colour would come exactly in the middle?
2. Who was the eleventh pharaoh of the 18th dynasty of Ancient Egypt?
3. Which mountain would you be climbing if you set up camp on the Khumbu Glacier?
4. Rearrange the letters 'PETNUNE' to get the name of a planet.
5. Traditionally, which animals pull the sledge of Santa Claus?
6. Which actress played the role of Rani in the 2014 film *Queen*?
7. Bankim Chandra Chattopadhyay wrote the national anthem of India: serious or joking?
8. Which is the only continent where bees are not found?

9. With which author would you associate the characters the Cheshire Cat and the Mad Hatter?
10. Which is the only city in the UK to have hosted the Summer Olympic Games thrice?

SET-7

1. Among Indians, who is the first to have played in more than 100 international football matches?
2. Who was the last British Viceroy of India?
3. All swans are white in colour: serious or joking?
4. According to the current rules, of which kind of wood must cricket bats be made?
5. Who played the male lead in the film *Ae Dil Hai Mushkil*?
6. Which chemical element has the atomic number 1?
7. The Ajanta Caves are situated at a distance of 107 km north of Aurangabad or Jamnagar?
8. Travelling from north to south, which of these would you cross first: the Jim Corbett National Park or the Gir Forest National Park?
9. In fiction, who employed the Baker Street Irregulars as informers?
10. For portraying which famous entrepreneur was Michael Fassbender nominated for an Oscar for Best Actor in 2016?

SET-8

1. Apples can also be green in colour: serious or joking?
2. Which animal did the first national stamp of Australia feature?
3. In which country is Taxila, a UNESCO World

Heritage Site, situated?

4. How many horns does the black rhinoceros have?

5. Mark Zuckerberg founded WhatsApp: serious or joking?

6. Which woman scientist wrote *Treatise on Radioactivity*?

7. The southernmost tip of which Indian union territory is only 150 km away from Sumatra, Indonesia?

8. The motto of which Indian organization is 'Industry, Impartiality, Integrity'?

9. In literature, with which day of the week did Robinson Crusoe's companion share his name?

10. Which famous politician is the daughter of Jagjivan Ram?

SET-9

1. Who, along with his daughter, Sonia Sanwalka, wrote his autobiography *The Race of My Life*?

2. Which organ of the human body consists of the outer epidermis and the inner dermis?

3. The name of which food item comes from the Greek word *makaria*?

4. While writing the names of Indian states alphabetically in English, the name of which state would come between Jharkhand and Kerala?

5. In English, how many colours of the rainbow have exactly six letters in their names?

6. Which empire in India came earlier: the Guptas or the Mauryas?

7. The Spanish word for tortoise is galápago: serious or joking?

8. In the Mahabharata, who was the most famous son of

Hiranyadhanush, the king of the foresters?
9. Who was the first prime minister of India to receive the Bharat Ratna?
10. Which director's last film was *Jab Tak Hai Jaan*?

SET-10

1. Of which epic are 'Aranya Kanda' and 'Kishkindha Kanda' sections?
2. In a game of chess, which is the only piece that cannot retreat?
3. Tooth enamel is not living and contains no nerves: serious or joking?
4. Which part of the egg contains more protein: the egg white or the yolk?
5. Which is the Inuit word for house?
6. The branch of which tree would you find on the emblem of the United Nations?
7. Which country's first president was Kemal Ataturk?
8. Which breed of dog is also known as German Shepherd?
9. In the world of computers, what is generally regarded as the largest wide-area network?
10. For which film did Vidya Balan win the Best Actress Award at the 2013 Filmfare Awards?

SET-11

1. Which deity's name would you find in the acronym, ISKCON?
2. To which country does golf player Vijay Singh belong: Fiji or India?
3. To which organ does the right side of the heart pump

the oxygen-poor blood that it collects?

4. If you were writing the names of Indian state alphabetically in English, which state would come between Punjab and Sikkim?

5. How many p's would you need to write the name of a country whose capital is Manila?

6. In 1924, which leader was appointed mayor of the Calcutta Municipal Corporation?

7. Which was the first creature to go into space?

8. The northern white rhinoceros is white in colour: serious or joking?

9. Which cartoon duck wears the middy blouse of a sailor suit and a sailor's hat?

10. Hamid Ansari is the current chairman of the Rajya Sabha: serious or joking?

SET-12

1. In the Ramayana, who was the mother of Lakshmana and Shatrughna?

2. For which team did Sachin Tendulkar play in the 2013 edition of the IPL?

3. If you are getting a cardiography done, which part of your body will be under examination?

4. While writing in English, the name of which planet in our solar system, apart from earth, starts with a vowel?

5. Neem, mango, peepal: which of these is the national tree of Bangladesh?

6. In India, to whose empire did Seleucus I send Megasthenes?

7. What is the state animal of Assam?

8. In 2002, how many planets were there in our solar system?
9. Which substance constitutes as much as 90 per cent of a tomato?
10. In India, whose birth anniversary is observed as Kisan Diwas?

SET-13

1. In Hindu mythology, who is also known as Bajrang Bali?
2. In the Indian Badminton League, in which city is the team Awadhe Warriors based?
3. In which part of the human body would you find the cardiac muscle?
4. In ancient Egypt, of which bird were the umbrellas used for protecting the nobility made?
5. On which day of the week did the year 2012 begin?
6. Qutbu'd-Din Aibak built only the first storey of the Qutb Minar: serious or joking?
7. Cuckoos lay their eggs only in the nests of crows: serious or joking?
8. In the acronym 'UFO', what does the letter 'U' stand for?
9. Of which Indian state was Vasundhara Raje the first woman chief minister?
10. Cardamom belongs to the ginger family: serious or joking?

SET-14

1. According to Hindu mythology, who is also known as Neelkanth?

2. Who is the only Indian cricketer to have received the Bharat Ratna?
3. Of which sense organ do contact lenses correct the defects?
4. In 2016, to which state in India was the GI tag for Kolhapuri chappals awarded?
5. Whose picture appears on a Pakistani Rs 50 note?
6. In 1924, which statue was designated a National Monument in the United States of America?
7. The name of which chemical element comes from the Latin word for coal?
8. From which state in north-eastern India comes the scientific name for the silkworm that produces muga silk?
9. Who is the first US president to have had a Twitter account while in office?
10. How many teaspoons make a tablespoon: 2 or 3?

SET-15

1. In the Ramayana, who unintentionally killed Shravan Kumar while hunting?
2. The nickname of which contemporary tennis ace is Djoker?
3. Which cone-shaped organ is located between the lungs and behind the breastbone?
4. Which was the world's fifth currency to get a symbol?
5. Traditionally, of which mythical creature's voice is the sound of thunder in the mountains of Bhutan believed to be?
6. Which heavenly body is known as *lune* in French and *Mond* in German?

7. In AD 14th through 17th centuries, which famous landmark did the Ming dynasty construct?
8. Only the male reindeer grows antlers: serious or joking?
9. In digital media, what is a blog an abbreviation of?
10. On whose death did Barack Obama tweet, 'Thank you, for showing us the power of one small step'?

SET-16

1. Which epic was born when Vyasa told Ganesh to write only after he had grasped the meaning?
2. In the IPL, what is the colour of the cap worn by the highest wicket-taker?
3. Which is the only finger of your hand that contains two bones?
4. Which city in Punjab connects the Bahadurgarh Fort and a type of loose salwar?
5. Mumbai is served by the Indira Gandhi International Airport: serious or joking?
6. Of which insect are painted ladies a species?
7. What weighs more: a kilogram of iron or a kilogram of feathers?
8. Which Indian city was formerly known as Anandavana, Kashika and Rudravasa?
9. Who has been the only woman prime minister of India so far?
10. The miners of which fuel are most commonly found with the black lung disease?

SET-17

1. How is the Mashriq al-adhkār in New Delhi better known?

2. In the Mahabharata, how many Pandavas were there?
3. Who is the first cricketer to play in 100 Test victories?
4. In humans, the earliest occurrence of a yawn happens right after the baby is born: serious or joking?
5. When writing the colours of the rainbow in English alphabetically, which colour appears last?
6. Of all the members of the UN, which country is listed last, alphabetically?
7. What do koalas do for 18–22 hours of a day: sleep or eat?
8. Which is the only planet of the solar system whose name ends with a vowel?
9. What is the symbol of the Samajwadi Party?
10. In the Ramayana, who was married to Urmila?

SET-18

1. The Arabica variety of what accounts for 80 per cent of its production?
2. Which Nobel Prize does the Karolinska Institute confer: Medicine, Physics or Economics?
3. After which dynasty is Ludhiana named?
4. Which country's national anthem is called 'The Thunder Dragon Kingdom'?
5. The scientific name of which animal is *Varanus komodoensis*?
6. Which is more dense: water at 4°C or ice at 0°C?
7. Of which mountain range is Guru Peak in Mount Abu the highest peak?
8. Besides New Delhi, how many Indian cities have a Supreme Court?

9. Bagheera and Baloo are Tarzan's friends: serious or joking?
10. In the Ramayana, who was Lava's brother?

SET-19

1. Sushi and pizza originated in the same country: serious or joking?
2. In a dictionary, the name of which month of the Gregorian calendar appears immediately before January?
3. Which explorer's smallest ship was Santa Clara, nicknamed Niṣa (Spanish for 'girl')?
4. In many churches in Armenia and Serbia, Christmas is celebrated in January: serious or joking?
5. How is the margosa tree better known to us?
6. Pure gold is twenty-four-carat gold: serious or joking?
7. What is the shape of barchan, the most common dune form on earth: crescent or star?
8. By which name is the artificial limb provided by Bhagwan Mahaveer Viklang Sahayata Samiti known?
9. In literature, what is the name of the little girl known for her adventures in Wonderland?
10. Who became the prime minister of India in 2014?

SET-20

1. With which baked food item can you relate small files which are stored on a user's computer?
2. The name of which member of the UN starts with a 'Y'?
3. With which human activity would you associate non-rapid eye movement and rapid eye movement?

4. The four novels of *The Twilight Saga* series are *Twilight, New Moon, Eclipse* and …
5. From which city did the British shift their capital to Delhi in 1911?
6. The term 'smog' comes from 'fog' and which other word?
7. Tamil Nadu is sometimes referred to as 'God's Own Country': serious or joking?
8. Which mountain peak is called 'Kumbh Karan Langúr' in Nepal?
9. Which president of India was immediately succeeded by India's first woman president?
10. Of which country is '.in' the internet code?

SET-21

1. Which fruit, also known as the Chinese gooseberry, is named after a bird from New Zealand?
2. Deepika Padukone played the title role in the 2016 film *Neerja*: serious or joking?
3. In which part of the body would you come across the conjunctiva?
4. In India, which machine has two units: the Control unit and the Balloting unit?
5. Which is the second largest lake in Jammu and Kashmir?
6. Which celestial body appears on the flag of China?
7. In India, what is the colour of the cover of a regular passport?
8. 'An eye for an eye only ends up making the whole world __________'. Fill in the blank to complete this quote by Mahatma Gandhi.

9. In the Mahabharata, which queen was born to the king of Panchala?
10. In computers, which sign is called 'Aapstert', meaning 'monkey's tail' in South Africa?

SET-22

1. Which is the odd one out: femur, mandible, fibula, tibia, patella?
2. Bombay Duck is a variety of duck: serious or joking?
3. In the USA, on which part of the body only can henna (*mehendi*) be legally used?
4. What was adopted as Japan's official monetary unit in 1871?
5. Which leader was born in Porbandar on 2 October 1869?
6. Which word connects an aromatic plant and a place where money is coined?
7. In which state of India is the satellite launch centre of Sriharikota located?
8. Through which ocean does the International Date Line pass?
9. In the Ramayana, in which king's palace did Sita grow up ?
10. In 2011, of which neighbouring country did Thein Sein become the first president?

SET-23

1. Steve Smith was appointed as the 45th Test captain of which team?
2. Does the brain or the heart control the rate at which we breathe?

3. For which part of the body is kohl usually used as make-up?
4. Find the connection: Greek mythology, a mountain and the first vertebra.
5. Which is heavier: two and a half kilograms or two thousand and sixty grams?
6. In Hindu mythology, with which sound do all mantras begin?
7. A scorpion has six legs: serious or joking?
8. Which colour appears between yellow and blue in the spectrum of colours?
9. In which state of India is Visakhapatnam a district?
10. The name of which egg preparation comes from a French word meaning 'knife blade'?

SET-24

1. In 2012, who defeated Israel's Boris Gelfand to win the World Chess Championship?
2. Rabies is transmitted to humans from animals: serious or joking?
3. Of which country's cuisine is sushi a staple rice dish?
4. How many months of the Gregorian calendar have the letter 'p' in them?
5. Which is the most widely spoken language in Brazil?
6. Which fort complex was built as the palace fort of Shahjahanabad, the new capital built by Shah Jahan?
7. Which letter immediately follows 'O' on a QWERTY keyboard?
8. In the Ramayana, who was the mother of Lava and Kusha?
9. Who was the first of the twelve men to have walked on

the surface of the earth's moon?

10. Who is married to educationist Devisingh Ransingh Shekhawat from Chhoti Losal?

SET-25

1. Which footballer was awarded the FIFA Ballon d'Or for 2014?
2. In the human body, what consists of a crown and one or more roots?
3. Which spice is called *zanjabil* in Arabic?
4. Which English word was coined by shortening the phrase 'God be with you'?
5. Which flower gets its name from the Swedish botanist Anders Dahl?
6. Which Mughal emperor was named Salim after Sheikh Salim Chishti?
7. In which country was the dobermann developed?
8. In the Mahabharata, who was the eldest of the Pandavas?
9. Who succeeded the first woman president of India?
10. A human heart can be transplanted: serious or joking?

ANSWERS

ART AND CULTURE

1. Shiv Kumar Sharma
2. Kathakali
3. Mandolin (Ghatam is a percussion instrument, and shehnai and bansuri are wind instruments.)
4. Diwali
5. White
6. Violin
7. Ravi Shankar
8. Mridangam
9. Bhimsen Joshi
10. Mukhda
11. Ravi Shankar. It has been written by his daughter Anoushka Shankar.
12. M.S. Subbulakshmi
13. Rice
14. Natraja
15. Zakir Hussain
16. Bharatanatyam
17. Odissi
18. One. The *Mona Lisa.*
19. Bismillah Khan
20. Amjad Ali Khan. Written by his sons Amaan Ali Bangash and Ayaan Ali Bangash.
21. Dalai Lama
22. M.F. Husain
23. Hornbill Festival
24. Nagaswaram

25. Madhya Pradesh

INDIA

1.   Bengali
2.   The shortest names of railway stations in India
3.   Exclamation mark
4.   Namaskar
5.   An ambulance
6.   Speaker, Lok Sabha
7.   Sanskrit
8.   Red Fort
9.   Asiatic lion
10. 12
11. Elephant
12. Diwali
13. 22 March
14. Post Offices
15. Weavers
16. CBI (Central Bureau of Investigation)
17. Destroyers
18. Uttar Pradesh. Seventy-five districts.
19. Bhojpuri. There are fifteen languages in the panel which appears on the reverse of the note.
20. Nashik
21. Sweets
22. Indira Gandhi
23. All India Radio
24. 10
25. Sikkim

MYTHOLOGY

1.   The first three Vedas
2.   Hanuman (Hanu meaning 'jawbone')

3. Gandhari
4. Lap
5. Buddha
6. Ravana
7. Sikhism
8. Karna
9. Duryodhan
10. Delhi
11. Sita
12. Eyes of the gods
13. Krishna
14. Ganesha
15. Vishnu
16. Saraswati
17. Sikhism. Nihangs (aka Akalis) are a very famous and prestigious armed Sikh order.
18. Chitragupta
19. Kaushalya
20. Musical instruments
21. Brahma
22. Bhima
23. Rama
24. Shiva
25. Vishwakarma

POLITICS

1. K.R. Narayanan
2. Angela Merkel
3. Pranab Mukherjee
4. Voting age
5. Bangladesh
6. Ministry of External Affairs
7. Parliament House

8. C. Rajagopalachari
9. Indira Gandhi (for a year from 1969 to 1970)
10. Riksdag
11. Jawaharlal Nehru
12. Afghanistan
13. Gulzarilal Nanda
14. Bangladesh
15. S. Radhakrishnan
16. Barack Obama
17. Russia
18. Morarji Desai
19. Shanti Van
20. Vijaya Lakshmi Pandit
21. Rajiv Gandhi
22. Bhutan
23. Nelson Mandela
24. Manmohan Singh
25. Atal Bihari Vajpayee

NATURE AND WILDLIFE-I

1. Pashmina
2. Palm tree
3. Vampire bat
4. Coconut
5. Iguana
6. Chicken
7. Dog
8. Gujarat
9. Salamander
10. Deer
11. *Born Free*
12. Gila Monster
13. Flamingo

14. Penguins
15. Giraffe
16. Cotton
17. Greyhound
18. Kiwi
19. Quinine. Quechua: *quina quina*, meaning 'bark of barks'.
20. The sound made by its wings
21. Spiders
22. Lion
23. Dolphin.
24. Eyes
25. Cheetah

NATURE AND WILDLIFE-II

1. Dinosaur. Greek: *deinos* 'terrible' + *sauros* 'lizard'.
2. Cheetah
3. Nepal
4. Great white shark
5. Rubber
6. Ants
7. Jaguar. Native American word: *yaguar*.
8. Kangaroos
9. Indian rhinoceros. It is known as *Rhinoceros unicornis*.
10. Hummingbird
11. Horse
12. Indian rhinoceros
13. Kiwi
14. Indian elephant
15. Peepal tree
16. Have tails. Apes do not have tails.
17. Marine snail
18. The Jim Corbett National Park

19. Bats
20. Ostrich
21. Yellow
22. Giraffe
23. Aardvarks
24. Pelican
25. Ostrich. Also because of its prominent eyes, sweeping eyelashes and its jolting walk, which are all similar to those of the camel.

MATHS-I

1.	35	Divide	7	Plus	14	Minus	11	=	8
2.	27	Plus	33	Multiply	2	Divide	8	=	15
3.	47	Minus	15	Plus	17	Multiply	1	=	49
4.	60	Minus	26	Multiply	5	Divide	17	=	10
5.	35	Multiply	3	Divide	15	Plus	21	=	28
6.	65	Minus	25	Divide	8	Multiply	11	=	55
7	46	Plus	34	Minus	35	Divide	5	=	9
8	15	Multiply	4	Minus	28	Plus	12	=	44

THE HUMAN BODY-I

1. Pupils
2. Quinine
3. Africa
4. Joints
5. Skin
6. Jaundice
7. Heart
8. Legs
9. Lymph
10. Vitamin C

11. Radius. One of the two large bones of the forearm.
12. Nervous system
13. Kidney
14. Stomach
15. Brain
16. Teeth
17. Pancreas
18. Liver
19. Stomach
20. Eye
21. Vertebral column
22. Mumps
23. Hypodermic
24. Small intestine
25. Blood sugar

GENERAL-I

1. A stamp. The three-skilling stamp was first issued in Sweden in 1855 and used in 1857 to mail a letter. Its last known sale price, in 2010, was $2,300,000.
2. Buddhism
3. Landing on the moon
4. Afghanistan
5. Chef
6. Arithmetic. Greek: *arithmós.*
7. Mulberry
8. Thailand
9. Education
10. Japan
11. 1 million
12. 12
13. Razia Sultan
14. Milk

15. Brass
16. Red
17. Andhra Pradesh
18. Maharashtra
19. C.V. Raman
20. Crore
21. Aquamarine. Latin: *aqua marinus*, meaning 'water of the sea', and referring to its sparkling ocean-like colour.
22. Sleeping positions
23. Greek
24. The president of India
25. Red

MATHS-II

1.	7	Multiply	9	Minus	32	Plus	18	=	49
2.	34	Multiply	5	Plus	16	Divide	31	=	6
3.	49	Divide	7	Plus	83	Multiply	0	=	0
4.	74	Plus	46	Divide	6	Minus	11	=	9
5.	39	Divide	13	Plus	95	Minus	69	=	29
6.	5	Plus	97	Minus	54	Divide	3	=	16
7.	84	Plus	13	Minus	88	Multiply	9	=	81
8.	85	Divide	5	Plus	25	Minus	23	=	19

GENERAL-II

1. Argentina
2. Mahatma and Kasturba Gandhi
3. Chillies. They are among the ten hottest chillies in the world.
4. Mother Teresa
5. Silkworm eggs
6. West Bengal
7. Never

8. Magsaysay Award. The Ramon Magsaysay Award is an annual award established in April 1957 to perpetuate former Philippine President Ramon Magsaysay's example of integrity in governance, courageous service to the people, and pragmatic idealism within a democratic society.
9. Spain
10. Aung San Suu Kyi
11. Zero. One crore is equal to 100 lakhs.
12. Diamond
13. Snake
14. C.N.R. Rao
15. Bhutan
16. Moustaches
17. Sarees. They are both very rich sarees, the former from Gujarat, the latter from Maharashtra.
18. S. Radhakrishnan
19. India
20. Labour. The acronym ILO stands for International Labour Organization.
21. Gangnam Style
22. Manna Dey
23. Fingerprints
24. Mountaineering
25. United Nations

HISTORY-I

1. Qutb Minar
2. Taj Mahal. The entire complex took approximately twenty years.
3. Shivaji
4. Mahatma Gandhi
5. Koh-i-Noor
6. Mark Antony

7. Darjeeling. After India's Independence in 1947, Darjeeling was merged with the state of West Bengal.
8. Panipat
9. The Mauryan Empire
10. Jantar Mantar, Jaipur
11. Shimla
12. Golden Temple
13. Peepal
14. Statue of Liberty
15. Chandragupta Maurya
16. Rashtrapati Bhavan
17. Alexander the Great
18. France
19. Ellora Caves
20. Babur
21. The United States of America.
22. Humayun's Tomb
23. Shivaji
24. Alexander the Great
25. The Eiffel Tower

HISTORY-II

1. Bairam Khan
2. Satyagrahi
3. Akbar
4. Tipu Sultan
5. Allahabad. They were Jawaharlal Nehru, Indira Gandhi, V.P. Singh.
6. Gujarat.
7. Statue of Liberty
8. Mahatma Gandhi.
9. Shah Jahan
10. India Gate

11. Rashtrapati Bhavan
12. Bhoodan
13. Florence Nightingale
14. Adolf Hitler
15. Eiffel Tower
16. Gol Gumbaz
17. A charkha (portable spinning wheel). Autographed in Hindi and English, a copy was shipped some 12,000 miles and personally delivered to Henry Ford by T.A. Raman, the London editor of the United Press of India, in Greenfield Village, Michigan.
18. Jantar Mantar
19. Greece
20. Mahatma Gandhi
21. October
22. Chetak. Chetak was the horse ridden by Maharana Pratap of Mewar at the Battle of Haldighati on 21 June 1576. Though mortally wounded himself, he carried his royal rider to safety before succumbing to his wounds.
23. Qutb Minar
24. Allahabad
25. Shah Jahan

MATHS-III

1.	62	Minus	46	Multiply	6	Divide	8	=	12
2.	14	Multiply	7	Minus	26	Plus	14	=	86
3.	27	Divide	3	Plus	54	Minus	42	=	21
4.	23	Multiply	7	Minus	75	Plus	11	=	97
5.	46	Minus	14	Multiply	2	Plus	6	=	70
6.	84	Minus	48	Plus	10	Divide	23	=	2

| 7. | 47 | Plus | 10 | Minus | 29 | Divide | 4 | = | 7 |
| 8. | 25 | Multiply | 4 | Plus | 25 | Minus | 68 | = | 57 |

SPORTS

1. Sachin Tendulkar
2. Dead ball
3. Marathon
4. Arm wrestling
5. Zimbabwe
6. Sania Mirza
7. 3
8. The Olympic flag with five rings.
9. Suresh Raina
10. Kerala
11. Ranjitsinhji. Sir K.S. Ranjitsinhji Vibhaji of Nawanagar, in whose honour, the first-class cricket tournament in India, the Ranji Trophy, was named and inaugurated in 1935.
12. Virat Kohli
13. Chennai Super Kings
14. Mark Boucher
15. Marathon. 26.2 miles
16. Yuvraj Singh. His father is Yograj Singh.
17. Ice hockey
18. Judo.
19. Sachin Tendulkar
20. Australia
21. Saina Nehwal
22. Blue card
23. Shooting
24. Metal ball
25. Billiards

LITERATURE-I

1. Spider-Man
2. *Treasure Island*
3. Buddhism
4. Ali Baba
5. A pound of his flesh
6. Firebolt
7. Pig
8. Jupiter
9. Malgudi
10. Mumbai. Then known as Bombay.
11. *3 Idiots*
12. Kabir. A doha is a lyrical verse-format which was extensively used by Indian poets of North India.
13. Cyborg
14. *A Brief History of Time,* written by Stephen Hawking. *Wings of Fire* is the autobiography of A.P.J. Abdul Kalam. *Long Walk to Freedom* is the autobiographical work of Nelson Mandela. *The Diary of a Young Girl* (also known as *The Diary of Anne Frank*) is the diary kept by Anne Frank while she was in hiding for two years with her family during the Nazi occupation of the Netherlands.
15. Ramayana
16. Hulk
17. Nepali
18. Hamlet
19. Iron Man
20. Unfriend
21. Alice's sister
22. Chacha Chaudhary
23. *Treasure Island*
24. Wolf
25. William Shakespeare. 'Fashionable' in *Troilus and Cressida,*

'foregone conclusion' in *Othello* and 'wild goose chase' in *Romeo and Juliet*.

LITERATURE-II

1. Gulliver
2. Great Expectations
3. Jaggu
4. *Panchatantra*
5. Dictionary. A 16th-century Latin word: *dictionarium manuale*.
6. Batman
7. Alice
8. A prison
9. Snowy
10. Dog
11. Satyajit Ray
12. William Shakespeare
13. The Phantom
14. *A Tale of Two Cities*
15. *Panchatantra*
16. Botanix
17. Colon. It consiss of two equal-sized dots, placed on the same vertical line.
18. Anagram. E.g., listen = silent.
19. Spider-Man. Gwen Stacy is Peter Parker's classmate and former girlfriend and the daughter of chief police officer George Stacy.
20. Plus
21. Positive influence on America's eating habits. The statue was erected to celebrate the boost given to the region's spinach-growing industry by Popeye: whenever he needs some extra strength, he downs a tin of spinach and instantly sprouts bulging biceps. Thereby, he convinced American

kids to eat spinach.

22. Mahatma Gandhi
23. Mickey Mouse
24. Aluminium
25. Green Lantern

ENTERTAINMENT

1. *Ra.One*
2. Ravi Shankar
3. *Deewar*
4. Amitabh Bachchan
5. Rajkumar Hirani
6. Salman Khan
7. Dhirubhai Ambani
8. Satyajit Ray
9. Abhishek Bachchan
10. Sonam Kapoor
11. Farhan Akhtar
12. Karan Johar
13. Rangda
14. Riteish Deshmukh
15. *Ice Age*
16. *Kuch Kuch Hota Hai*
17. Lord Voldemort
18. *Dilwale Dulhania Le Jayenge*
19. Farhan Akhtar
20. *Toy Story*
21. *Bunty Aur Babli*
22. Jackie Chan
23. Farah Khan
24. Ranbir Kapoor

25. Rahul Bose. In 1998, Bose was part of the first Indian national rugby team to play in an international event, the Asian Rugby Football Union Championship.

SCIENCE AND TECHNOLOGY-I

1. Earth
2. WhatsApp
3. Saturn
4. Dogs in space.
5. Coffee pot
6. Stethoscope. Greek: *stethos* (breast) + *skopein* (to explore)
7. English (Pirate)
8. Neptune
9. John Logie Baird
10. Iodine
11. W
12. Ron Klein
13. Encryption
14. Selfie
15. Blue
16. C.V. Raman
17. Temple Run
18. Reflex
19. Megabyte
20. Microwave oven. One day, while building magnetrons, Spencer was standing in front of an active radar set when he noticed the candy bar he had in his pocket had melted. He continued to experiment using food, and created the first microwave oven by attaching a high density electromagnetic field generator to an enclosed metal box.
21. F4
22. Arrows. Four arrow keys arranged in an inverted T formation between the typing keys and the numeric keypad

move the cursor on the screen in small increments.

23. Parasite. Greek: *parasitos* = 'person eating at another's table', from *para-* (alongside) + *sitos* (food).
24. Hashtag
25. Galileo Galilei

MATHS-IV

1.	19	Multiply	5	Minus	26	Divide	3	=	23
2.	18	Divide	9	Multiply	36	Minus	47	=	25
3.	13	Multiply	7	Minus	31	Divide	3	=	20
4.	58	Minus	12	Plus	34	Divide	16	=	5
5.	15	Multiply	7	Minus	75	Plus	26	=	56
6.	42	Plus	16	Divide	2	Multiply	3	=	87
7.	36	Minus	18	Multiply	3	Plus	35	=	89
8.	26	Plus	44	Minus	35	Divide	7	=	5

SCIENCE AND TECHNOLOGY-II

1. Silver
2. Total solar eclipse
3. English
4. Radium
5. S. Chandrasekhar
6. LCD
7. Silver
8. Marie Curie
9. China
10. Neptune
11. Laika. American reporters dubbed her Muttnik as a pun on Sputnik.
12. Linux
13. Chemistry
14. C.V. Raman. During a voyage to Europe in 1921,

he noticed the blue colour of glaciers and of the Mediterranean Sea.

15. Ctrl + S
16. Neptune
17. Jupiter
18. Computer mouse
19. Albert Einstein
20. Gold
21. Insulin
22. Albert Einstein. Einsteinium is a synthetic element with the symbol 'Es'.
23. Spain
24. Nobelium—named after Alfred Nobel, the inventor of dynamite and benefactor of science.
25. Neptune

GEOGRAPHY-I

1. The sunrise seen from Mount Fuji.
2. Assam
3. Contour line
4. Africa
5. Mauritius
6. Antarctica
7. Pakistan
8. Robinson Crusoe Island. Alexander Selkirk was a Scottish privateer and Royal Navy officer who spent more than four years as a castaway after being marooned by his captain on this uninhabited island in the South Pacific Ocean.
9. Myanmar
10. China
11. Archipelago
12. Chhattisgarh
13. Narmada

14. S
15. Asia
16. Bangladesh
17. Godavari
18. Brahmaputra
19. Red Sea
20. Bihar
21. Yash Chopra. He shot so many films in Switzerland that a lake in the Alpenrausch, a favourite shooting location of his, was christened Chopra Lake.
22. Sri Lanka
23. Sutlej
24. Sahara
25. Godavari. It is so called because of its large size and extent among the peninsular rivers.

GEOGRAPHY-II

1. Antarctica
2. Jakarta
3. Bhutan
4. La Paz
5. Gujarat
6. Cumulus. Latin: *cumulus*.
7. Maldives
8. Subhas Chandra Bose
9. South America
10. Andaman and Nicobar Islands
11. Mount Fuji
12. Jammu and Kashmir
13. Dunes
14. Uttarakhand
15. Philippines
16. Sri Lanka

17. Australia
18. Goa
19. Haridwar
20. Kilimanjaro
21. China. That is one of the Chinese names for the Great Wall of China.
22. Mount Everest
23. Baghdad
24. The Siachen Glacier
25. Aurora Borealis. Auroras are fantastic displays of light that occur in the upper atmosphere at both poles. They are known as Aurora Borealis in the north and as Aurora Australis in the south. Pierre Gassendi applied the name 'auroras' to them, after Aurora the goddess of dawn in Roman mythology, and the Greek name for the north wind, Boreas.

FOOD

1. Aniseed
2. Spanish
3. Orange
4. Cabbage. Old French: *chef*.
5. Jalebi
6. Potato
7. Uttar Pradesh. It derives its name from Kakori, a small town on the outskirts of Lucknow in Uttar Pradesh.
8. Poppy seeds
9. Dhansak
10. Besan
11. Gulab Jamun. Lalmohan is a Bengali dessert.
12. Mango
13. Pasta
14. Tibet

15. Basmati rice
16. Clove
17. Rice
18. Semolina/rawa/suji
19. Bihar
20. Saffron
21. Bangladesh
22. Coconut
23. Laddoo
24. Banana
25. Apple

BUZZER ROUND

SET-1

1. Twentieth
2. Camel
3. Marie Curie
4. Joking. It was adopted in 1950.
5. *Moby-Dick*
6. Madhya Pradesh
7. Julius Caesar
8. C. Rajagopalachari
9. Dhyan Chand. 29 August.
10. Tansen

SET-2

1. Joking. It is green.
2. Madurai
3. 7. *Saat Hindustani.*
4. Serious
5. Albert Einstein
6. Aurangzeb

7. 12
8. Malgudi
9. Kachchh. It is situated in Gujarat.
10. Andre Agassi

SET-3

1. Indian Navy
2. Hyderabad
3. Joking. A *tapir* is a large, herbivorous mammal, similar in shape to a pig, inhabiting jungle and forest regions of South America.
4. *Mangal Pandey: The Rising*
5. Archimedes. The Archimedes screw was a device historically used for transferring water from a low-lying body of water into irrigation ditches.
6. Father
7. The Constitution of India. It was adopted on 26 November 1949, and came into force on 26 January 1950.
8. Dal Lake
9. Anne Frank
10. Manchester United

SET-4

1. Joking. They were the military, nobility and officer caste of medieval and early-modern Japan.
2. Tutankhamun. An Egyptian pharaoh of the 18th dynasty who, since the discovery of his tomb, has been colloquially referred to as King Tut.
3. Joking. Birds have beaks which vary significantly in size, shape, color and texture.
4. Sonakshi Sinha
5. Parachute. French: *parachute*, from *para-* (protection against) + *chute* (fall)

6. Blue
7. Joking. It is shaped like the leaf of the peepal tree.
8. Literature. He was awarded it for 'his mastery of historical and biographical description as well as for brilliant oratory in defending exalted human values'.
9. Spain
10. A

SET-5

1. Bhutan
2. The Great Wall of China
3. Joking. Jellyfish are soft-bodied, free-swimming, aquatic animals with a gelatinous umbrella-shaped bell and trailing tentacles.
4. Japan
5. Lead
6. Queen Victoria's. It was formerly known as the Victoria Terminus.
7. Karnataka
8. Yamuna
9. Serious. It is a title given to William Shakespeare, who was born and buried in Stratford-upon-Avon, England. A bard is a poet.
10. The French Open, a major tennis tournament held over two weeks between late May and early June at the Stade Roland Garros in Paris, France.

SET-6

1. Orange
2. Tutankhamun
3. Mount Everest. The Khumbu Glacier is located in the Khumbu region of north-eastern Nepal between Mount Everest and the Lhotse-Nuptse ridge.

4. Neptune
5. Reindeer
6. Kangana Ranaut
7. Joking. Rabindranath Tagore wrote the national anthem of India.
8. Antarctica
9. Lewis Caroll, in the book *Alice's Adventures in Wonderland.*
10. London. In 1908, 1948 and 2012.

SET-7

1. Bhaichung Bhutia
2. Lord Louis Mountbatten
3. Joking. The northern hemisphere species of swan have pure white plumage but the southern hemisphere species are mixed black and white.
4. Willow
5. Ranbir Kapoor
6. Hydrogen
7. Aurangabad
8. The Jim Corbett National Park
9. Sherlock Holmes. The Baker Street Irregulars are fictional characters who appear in various Sherlock Holmes stories, as street children who are employed by Holmes as intelligence agents.
10. Steve Jobs. An American entrepreneur, businessman, inventor and industrial designer, he was the co-founder, chairman and chief executive of Apple Inc.

SET-8

1. Serious. They can also be yellow, pink, or green.
2. Kangaroo
3. Pakistan
4. 2

5. Joking. WhatsApp was founded by Jan Koum and Brian Acton. Mark Zuckerberg is the chairman, chief executive officer and co-founder of Facebook.
6. Marie Curie
7. Andaman and Nicobar Islands. The southernmost island is Great Nicobar.
8. CBI (Central Bureau of Investigation)
9. Friday. Friday is one of the main characters of Daniel Defoe's 1719 novel *Robinson Crusoe*. Robinson Crusoe names the man, with whom he cannot at first communicate, Friday because they first meet on that day.
10. Meira Kumar. She is an Indian politician and a five-time Member of Parliament. She was elected unopposed as the first woman Speaker of Lok Sabha and served from 2009–2014.

SET-9

1. Milkha Singh
2. Skin. It is the largest external organ.
3. Macaroni. Actually, from Italian: *maccaroni* (now usually spelt *maccheroni*); from late Greek: *makaria* (food made from barley).
4. Karnataka
5. 4
6. The Mauryas. The Mauryan dynasty ruled from 321 BC–185 BC, while the Guptas ruled from about AD 20–AD 540.
7. Serious
8. Ekalavya
9. Jawaharlal Nehru
10. Yash Chopra

SET-10

1. The Ramayana

2. Pawn
3. Serious
4. The yolk
5. Igloo
6. Olive tree
7. Turkey
8. Alsatian
9. Internet
10. *Kahaani*

SET-11

1. Krishna. ISKCON sands for The International Society for Krishna Consciousness, also known as the Hare Krishna movement.
2. Fiji
3. Lungs
4. Rajasthan
5. It is Philippine.
6. Subhas Chandra Bose
7. A Russian dog. The name of the dog was Laika.
8. Joking. It is actually more of a battleship grey or, sometimes, a latte-brown.
9. Donald Duck
10. Serious. According to the Constitution of India, Ansari, as Vice-President of the Republic, also serves ex officio as Chairman of the Rajya Sabha.

SET-12

1. Sumitra
2. Mumbai Indians
3. Heart
4. Uranus
5. Mango

6. Chandragupta Maurya's
7. Indian rhinoceros
8. 9
9. Water
10. Chaudhary Charan Singh's. He was the fifth prime minister and a kisan leader. Kisan Diwas is celebrated on 23 December, his birth anniversary.

SET-13

1. Hanuman
2. Lucknow
3. Heart
4. Peacock
5. Sunday
6. Serious. Three more storeys were added by his successor and son-in-law, Shamsu'd-Din Iltutmish.
7. Joking
8. Unidentified. UFO stands for 'unidentified flying object', any apparent anomaly in the sky that is not identifiable as a known object or phenomenon.
9. Rajasthan. Vasundhara Raje was sworn in as Rajasthan's first woman chief minister in 2003.
10. Serious. Ginger is a flowering plant, which belongs to the family Zingiberaceae, to which also belong turmeric, cardamom and galangal.

SET-14

1. Shiva
2. Sachin Tendulkar
3. Eyes
4. Maharashtra. A geographical indication (GI) is a name or sign used on certain products to correspond to a specific geographical location or origin.

5. Muhammad Ali Jinnah
6. Statue of Liberty
7. Carbon. Latin: *carbo*.
8. Assam. Muga silk is the product of the silkworm, *Antheraea assamensis,* endemic to Assam.
9. Barack Obama
10. 3 tsp

SET-15

1. Dasharatha
2. Novak Djokovic. In English, Djokovic is pronounced as Joke-a-vitch, hence he is 'The Joker' or 'Djoker'.
3. Heart
4. Rupee. The other four are: the US dollar, the euro, the yen and the British pound.
5. Dragon
6. Moon
7. The Great Wall of China
8. Joking. The males of almost all deer species grow antlers, to battle for females. Reindeer is the only species whose females grow antlers to forage for and to defend food in small patches of cleared snow.
9. Weblog
10. Neil Armstrong. 'Neil Armstrong was a hero not just of his time, but of all time,' Barack Obama said via Twitter. 'Thank you, Neil, for showing us the power of one small step.'

SET-16

1. The Mahabharata
2. Purple
3. Thumb
4. Patiala. Bahadurgarh Fort is a historical fort, built in the

year 1658, 6 kilometres away from Patiala city. A Patiala salwar, which has its roots in Patiala City, is different from the usual salwar in that it requires double the length of material to get stitched, and has many pleats.

5. Joking. It is in New Delhi. The Mumbai Metropolitan Area is served by the Chhatrapati Shivaji International Airport, formerly known as Sahar International Airport.
6. Butterfly
7. They weigh the same
8. Varanasi. Anandavana meant 'the forest of bliss'; Kashika meant 'the shining one' referring to the light of Shiva; Rudravasa was 'the place where Shiva (Rudra) resides'.
9. Indira Gandhi; for a year from 1970 to 1971.
10. Coal. Black lung disease is caused by long exposure to coal dust. It is common in coal miners and others who work with coal.

SET-17

1. Lotus Temple. Mashriq al-adhkār (in Arabic: 'the place where the uttering of the name of God arises at dawn) is the temple or house of worship in the Bahā'ī faith.
2. 5
3. Ricky Ponting
4. Joking. It happens in the mother's womb. It is not clear why unborn babies yawn; the movement may be related to the maturation of their central nervous systems.
5. Yellow
6. Zimbabwe
7. Sleep
8. Neptune
9. Cycle
10. Lakshmana

SET-18

1. Coffee
2. Medicine or Physiology
3. Lodhi
4. Bhutan. Dzongkha or Bhutanese: Druk tsendhen (The Thunder Dragon Kingdom).
5. Komodo dragon
6. Water at 4°C
7. Aravalli Range
8. None
9. Joking. They are Mowgli's friends.
10. Kusha

SET-19

1. Joking. Sushi is from Japan and pizza from Italy.
2. February
3. Christopher Columbus
4. Serious. The Armenian Apostolic Church celebrates Christmas on 6 January. In Serbia, the Orthodox Church celebrates it on 7 January.
5. Neem tree
6. Serious
7. Crescent
8. Jaipur Foot
9. Alice
10. Narendra Modi

SET-20

1. Cookie
2. Yemen
3. Sleep
4. *Breaking Dawn*
5. Calcutta (now known as Kolkata)

6. Smoke
7. Joking. In India, it is Kerala that is known by that title. The expression was first used to describe Yorkshire. Thereafter, it has been used in association with other territories across the world.
8. Kanchenjunga
9. A.P.J. Abdul Kalam. Succeeded by Pratibha Patil.
10. India

SET-21

1. Kiwi
2. Joking. Sonam Kapoor played the lead role in *Neerja*.
3. Eyes
4. Electronic Voting Machines or EVM
5. Dal Lake. Wular Lake is the largest lake in Jammu and Kashmir.
6. Star
7. Navy blue
8. Blind
9. Draupadi
10. At the rate of or @

SET-22

1. Mandible. The rest are all bones in the leg. The mandible is the jawbone.
2. Joking. It is a kind of fish.
3. Hair. Henna is approved only for use as a hair dye—not for direct application to the skin, The Food and Drug Administration (USA) has received reports of injuries to the skin from products marketed as henna.
4. Yen
5. Mahatma Gandhi
6. Mint

7. Andhra Pradesh. The Satish Dhawan Space Centre is located on Sriharikota, a barrier island off the Bay of Bengal coast.
8. Pacific Ocean
9. Janaka
10. Myanmar (formerly known as Burma)

SET-23

1. Australia
2. The brain
3. Eyes
4. Atlas. i) In Greek mythology, Atlas was a Titan who, with his brother, sided with the Titans in their war against the Olympians. The Titans lost, and Atlas was condemned to hold up the sky for eternity. ii) The Atlas Mountains are a series of mountain ranges in northwestern Africa. iii) The atlas is the topmost vertebra. It is named for Atlas of Greek mythology, because it supports the globe of the head.
5. Two and a half kilograms. That is, 2,500 grams. Hence, it is heavier than 2,060 grams.
6. Om
7. Joking. It has eight legs.
8. Green. The division used by Isaac Newton, in his colour wheel, was: red, orange, yellow, green, blue, indigo and violet; a mnemonic for this order is 'Roy G. Biv'.
9. Andhra Pradesh
10. Omelette. From *la lemelle*. This word, literally meaning, 'the blade of a sword or knife' (because an omelette is flat and thin like a blade), was borrowed into early French. Then the word *lemelle* underwent many linguistic changes, and finally, entered into the English language as 'omelette'.

SET-24

1. Viswanathan Anand
2. Serious
3. Japan. Sushi is a preparation of cooked vinegared rice, combined with varied ingredients, such as seafood, vegetables, meat, fish and, occasionally, tropical fruits.
4. 2. April and September.
5. Portuguese
6. Red Fort
7. P
8. Sita
9. Neil Armstrong
10. Pratibha Patil

SET-25

1. Cristiano Ronaldo
2. Tooth
3. Ginger
4. Goodbye
5. Dahlia
6. Jahangir
7. Germany. The dobermann was originally developed around 1890 by Karl Friedrich Louis Dobermann, a tax collector from Germany.
8. Yudhishthira
9. Pranab Mukherjee
10. Serious. The world's first adult human heart transplant was performed by a South African cardiac surgeon, Christiaan Barnard, in December 1967.

www.ingramcontent.com/pod-product-compliance
Lightning Source LLC
Chambersburg PA
CBHW051054250726
48656CB00001B/297